A LOAF OF
BREAD

A LOAF OF BREAD

Bread in History, in the Kitchen and on the Table: Recipes and Traditions

GAIL DUFF

PUBLISHED BY THE READER'S DIGEST ASSOCIATION LIMITED
LONDON

A READER'S DIGEST BOOK

Published by The Reader's Digest Association Limited
11 Westferry Circus
Canary Wharf
London E14 4HE

ISBN 0 276 42347 X

This book was designed and produced by
Quarto Publishing plc
The Old Brewery
6 Blundell St
London N7 9BH

Art editor: Sally Bond
Designer: Liz Brown
Editor: Nancy Terry
Copy editor: Madelaine Weston
Managing editor: Sally MacEachern
Picture researcher: Zoe Holtermann
Photographer: Iain Bagwell, Colin Bowling
Illustrator: Jane Smith
Home Economist: Gail Duff
Stylist: Rachel Jukes
Assistant art director: Penny Cobb
Art director: Moira Clinch
Editorial director: Pippa Rubinstein

Typeset in Great Britain by Central Southern Typesetters, Eastbourne
Manufactured in Hong Kong by Regent Publishing Services Ltd
Printed in Singapore by Star Standard Industries (Pte) Ltd

CONTENTS

INTRODUCTION

THERE ARE FEW THINGS IN THE WORLD SO SATISFYING AS BREAD. IT HAS BEEN A STAPLE FOOD IN MANY COUNTRIES FOR THOUSANDS OF YEARS AND IT WILL PROBABLY BE SO FOR THOUSANDS MORE. THE SMELL OF BAKING BREAD IS ONE OF THE MOST ENTICING SCENTS IN THE WORLD.

Demeter, seen here with her sickle and sheaf of wheat and poppies, was the Greek goddess of the harvest. In rescuing Persepone from the underworld, she ensured that spring would always return after winter.

Early settlers in America at first found it hard to grow European varieties of wheat. Today, America is one of the biggest grain producers in the world.

Bread has been so important to human existence that, in the Bible and in many classical stories, the word itself is often synonymous with 'food'. In most English-speaking countries, 'bread' and 'dough' are colloquial expressions for money.

Because in early history bread was literally the 'staff of life', it is at the centre of many religious customs and festivals. In some parts of the world, a goddess or god, or the giver and taker away of life, was associated with corn, because people's very existence depended on this grain. The Aztecs worshipped a corn god, and in ancient Greece Demeter was the goddess of the harvest and her daughter Persephone the corn maiden. In other countries, the planting, growth and harvesting of grain represented the continuing cycle of birth, life and death. Even now, there is still a certain magic about the life cycle of the crop. Ploughing opens up welcoming tracts of earth, ready to receive the seed. Gradually the earth is covered in green as the young stalks grow. When the grain is mature, the landscape turns golden, the harvesting starts, and the age-old process begins again.

Whatever the country or the religious beliefs, there was always great celebration when the harvest was safely gathered. It was the culmination of a year's hard work, ploughing, sowing and reaping, and often provided reassurance that a community would survive the coming winter. Worldwide, people still celebrate the safe gathering of the harvest.

Depending on the types of grain grown, every country has its preferences for different types of flour and different baking methods, born of long historical associations and climatic differences. The corn (maize) bread of the United States, for example, was first made by the Native Americans and unknown to the first settlers, who continued to stoically plant their seed corn before discovering that the native maize thrived better than the imported cereal crops. Bannocks and oatcakes became popular in Scotland because they were easy to make on flat stones or iron griddles in cottages that had open fires and no ovens.

Bread and cheese, chapatis and lentils, tortillas and beans, bagels and smoked fish are classic combinations, born of different climates,

6

styles of farming and ways of life. Almost every country in the world has its own classic bread recipe, often created in homes and eaten locally at first, but later taken across continents by travellers to become internationally known and commercially available.

When you eat bread you are taking part in a cycle that begins with sowing the seed and ends with loaves being sold. You may not feel a connection with the farming end of bread production, but you can still take part in the cycle by buying the flour and making your own bread. In doing so, you will be carrying on a skill that has been practised for millennia. You, too, can experience the feel of the dough in your hands, the pleasure when the dough begins to rise, the tantalising smell as the loaves cook and the satisfaction in seeing your family and friends happy and well-fed.

Bread-making is special. With a few simple ingredients and a dollop of enthusiasm, you end

Loaf Givers

Cookery means the knowledge of Medea and of Circe and of Helen and of the Queen of Sheba. It means the knowledge of all herbs and fruits and balms and spices, and all that is healing and sweet in the fields and groves and savoury in meats. It means carefulness and inventiveness and willingness and readiness of appliances. It means the economy of your grandmothers and the science of the modern chemist; it means much testing and no wasting; it means English thoroughness and French art and Arabian hospitality; and, in fine, it means that you are to be perfectly and always ladies – loaf givers.

JOHN RUSKIN, 1819–1900

Special harvest loaves are baked all over the world. Many are used to decorate places of worship at services where thanks is given for a successful harvest.

up with a beautiful, sweet-smelling, delicious food that will not only provide you with energy, vitamins and minerals, but also will be an easy accompaniment to other foods.

Making bread is not difficult. All you need are a few basic ingredients and the patience to wait for the dough to rise. You don't need expensive equipment, and for some recipes you don't even need an oven. It doesn't have to be time-consuming either. You can use a bread machine if you are in a particular hurry, either to make the entire loaf or just to knead the bread. Even if you stick entirely to traditional methods, you can leave the dough to rise for an hour, after the initial mixing and kneading before shaping it.

When you are making bread for the first time, start with the basic recipe. Once you have mastered it, experiment by changing the type of flour or try different yeasts to see which one suits you best. Experiment with shapes and sizes of loaves. Soon, you will have a customised bread recipe that suits your oven, your available ingredients and your taste. Then you can confidently move on to recipes with more ingredients or more complicated methods.

Pilgrims, such as these, crossed the Atlantic in their small and flimsy boats taking wheat, rye and barley to North America.

7

THE HISTORY OF BREAD

THROUGHOUT MUCH OF THE WORLD, THE DEVELOPMENT OF BREAD AND THE RISE OF CIVILISATIONS HAVE GONE HAND-IN-HAND. ALMOST EVERYWHERE PEOPLE SETTLED, GRAIN WAS GROWN, AND WHEREVER THESE PEOPLE HAVE TRAVELLED, THE KNOWLEDGE OF GROWING GRAIN AND BAKING BREAD HAS GONE WITH THEM AND CONTRIBUTED TO THEIR SURVIVAL IN NEW LANDS.

The ancient Egyptians grew corn in the fertile land around the Nile Delta. Their planting and harvesting techniques were unchanged for centuries.

The seeds of wild grasses were first recognised as a nutritious food around 10 000 BC, when people lived by hunting and gathering. This happened more or less simultaneously in Europe and the Middle East and also on the plains of what is now the USA.

In the region of the Andes, an ancestor of maize was gathered alongside wild tomatoes and potatoes. In different parts of the world, grains were ground with stones and mixed with water, and eaten as a kind of porridge.

Around 9000 BC permanent settlements were established on the grassy areas of the Middle East and people first learned that if some seed were retained from the grain harvest and re-sown, a more regular supply of food could be ensured. With the development of settled – as opposed to nomadic – living, people had more time to experiment and it was discovered that the porridge mixture could be cooked in small amounts on hot, flat stones to make small cakes of unleavened bread. These were the ancestors of all the flat breads that we know today, such as tortillas, chapatis and Ethiopian *injera*.

Around 6000 BC bread-making wheats with larger grains and, eventually, a high gluten content were developed. Their use soon spread,

Fannie Merritt Farmer

Miss Fannie Merritt Farmer was born in the eastern United States around the middle of the nineteenth century. For some years she ran the Boston Cookery School, where she taught young women how to make all the classic American dishes such as pumpkin pie, chowder, planked steak and boiled dinner. Her book, The Original Boston Cooking School Cookbook, *was first published in 1896, and it was full of the basic recipes and common sense that had made her school so popular. By the time she died in 1915, her book had sold six million copies and the name Fannie Farmer had become synonymous with good cooking and good housewifery.*

Fannie Farmer's chapter on 'Bread and Bread-making' includes details about types of wheat, milling, flour and raising agents, together with the basic principles for making an excellent loaf, all of which are still relevant today.

'The study of bread-making,' she said, 'is of no slight importance, and deserves more attention than it receives. Considering its great value, it seems unnecessary and wrong to find poor bread on the table.'

Eliza Acton

In nineteenth-century England, particularly around the 1850s, the price and availability of wheat for bread-making varied tremendously. As a result, bakers commonly adulterated flour – or in their terms, 'improved' it – with such ingredients as potatoes, alum, chalk and bone meal, which could both bulk out the flour and improve the appearance of an inferior loaf.

Conditions in many bakeries were far from hygienic, and there are shocking descriptions of flour being kept in the damp, 'and, above all, sickly, perspiring men in contact with our food'.

All this so appalled English cook Eliza Acton that, in 1857, she was moved to write The English Bread Book, *exposing the tricks and bad practices of the bakery trade and urging all housewives to bake their own bread.*

She gives details of flours, raising agents and methods, recipes such as 'Excellent Suffolk Bread', 'Good Family Bread' and 'The Frugal Housewife's Brown Bread' and tips such as 'The Tests of Well-Made Bread'. All the instructions are clear and concise and apply just as much today as when they were first written.

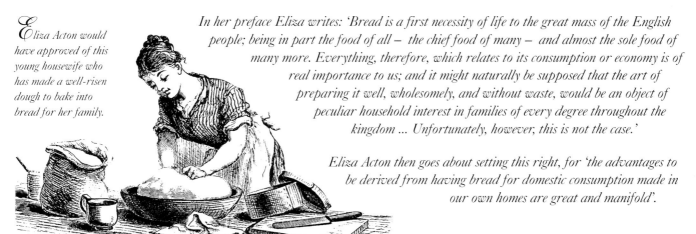

Eliza Acton would have approved of this young housewife who has made a well-risen dough to bake into bread for her family.

In her preface Eliza writes: 'Bread is a first necessity of life to the great mass of the English people; being in part the food of all – the chief food of many – and almost the sole food of many more. Everything, therefore, which relates to its consumption or economy is of real importance to us; and it might naturally be supposed that the art of preparing it well, wholesomely, and without waste, would be an object of peculiar household interest in families of every degree throughout the kingdom ... Unfortunately, however, this is not the case.'

Eliza Acton then goes about setting this right, for 'the advantages to be derived from having bread for domestic consumption made in our own homes are great and manifold'.

9

people were better fed and the early civilisations began to develop. Then, by trial and error, it was learned that a dough left for a long time in a warm place would start to ferment and that this process made the finished result more palatable. This must have been the way that sourdough breads originated.

It was the Egyptians who first discovered and developed the use of yeast, giving rise to the breads we know today. The Greeks called the Egyptians *artophagoi*, meaning 'the bread eaters', and part of the wages of the Egyptian troops was 2kg (4lb) of wheat and barley bread per day. However, only the rich were able to eat yeasted bread and even this was never perfect. One of the Pharaohs hanged his baker because of the poor quality of his loaves.

In remote places such as the Isle of Skye in Scotland, where there were no shops and few local mills, wheat for bread-making had to be ground at home. These nineteenth-century crofters are shown using a hand mill.

In ancient settlements, such as this one on the west coast of Ireland, small, flat cakes made of mixed grains and seeds would have been baked on hot stones by the fire.

By about 1000 BC in ancient Greece, it seems that barley was the most popular grain for making bread, but by 450 BC wheat was the staple grain. Bread was raised by keeping a batch of dough from the last baking to start the next, and rich people were able to add honey, milk, pepper and sweet wine to the dough to vary the textures and flavours.

At the same time, different types of wheat and barley were being developed in Britain and western Europe. Small hearth-cakes found in Glastonbury, England and dating from 1 BC contain wheat, barley, wild oats and the seeds of a wild plant called *orache*.

The first domed ovens were used in Europe during the Iron Age. Yeast from brewing beer was used for the dough, producing breads more like those of today.

For a long time, the Romans preferred a thick porridge called *puls* to bread. Eventually they took to baking, but are reputed to have been bad at it. Early Roman bread was heavy and difficult to digest, but, towards the end of the

Roman era, the rich demanded fine white bread, thus establishing an attitude that was to last for almost 1000 years: that white bread was for the wealthy and brown for the poor.

In Saxon times, bread made from a mixture of wheat and rye, called *maslin* bread, was the most common. Made at home, it was usually unleavened and baked on a hearth stone. There were, however, professional bakers who made leavened bread.

In medieval times, all over Europe, the poor used what grains they could get, together with weed seeds, ground beans or chestnuts and even, in some places, ground tree bark, while the rich demanded the whitest bread possible. By the fourteenth and fifteenth centuries there were many types of bread available, including those enriched with butter, milk and eggs. There were also a number of laws and regulations governing quality. In sixteenth-century Europe, better quality grains were favoured in different areas and so fewer of the bulking ingredients had to be used. Bread was getting better.

At the end of the fifteenth century, Christopher Columbus found maize in what is now Cuba and took seeds back to Spain. He also found tribes in the Bahamas making bread from the fermented seeds of the zamia plant. The Spanish discovered cassava bread in the same area and took the plant to Africa, where it soon became a staple food. When Cortez invaded Mexico, the Spaniards planted wheat, and a colony established by Walter Raleigh first grew wheat in North Carolina in 1585.

From the seventeenth century onwards, wheat-growing, milling and baking improved on both sides of the Atlantic, and breads and methods were devised to suit the new conditions. American settlers learned how to make corn breads. Trekkers in South Africa devised a way of baking in a cast-iron pot.

During the nineteenth century, greater quantities of commercial bread were being made and bread was often adulterated with ingredients such as chalk and bone meal. This caused Fannie Farmer in America and Eliza Acton and William Cobbett in England to speak out for home baking.

In 1856, John Dauglish, an English chemist, found a method for aerating bread dough, but bakers were reluctant to use the idea until 1900.

The twentieth century has seen a rise in the status and quality of bread. For many years

In the Middle Ages, ploughing and sowing had changed very little since Egyptian times. Wooden ploughs were drawn across the fields by horses and the seed was sown by hand. Harvesting was done with sickles.

In fourteenth-century England, a baker who made underweight loaves was punished by being drawn through the streets with a loaf around his neck, and was placed in the pillory.

white, sliced bread was the most popular. It was new, convenient and reasonably priced. Everyone could now have pure white bread. Then, in the 1960s, it was discovered that white may not be the healthiest option and wholewheat bread became fashionable and, for a while, was more expensive than white bread.

Approaching the next millennium, we now have the perfect situation. In many countries, bread is reasonably priced and well-made and there is a choice of varieties. It is now often easy to find Italian ciabatta, Indian nan, French baguettes, Scandinavian pumpernickel and English muffins. Some are wholewheat, some white and some are a mixture. Like many countries of the world, bread has become extremely cosmopolitan.

A large proportion of the bread bought today is made in factories. This ensures loaves of an even size, weight and texture, but many people prefer hand-made bread.

William Cobbett

William Cobbett, 1762–1835, is now best known for his book Rural Rides, *in which he described his journeys through eighteenth-century England, but during his lifetime he was probably best known for his* Cottage Economy, *which, soon after it was published in 1823, found its way into many country kitchens.*

It was a book full of information for 'cottagers' who kept their own cows, pigs, sheep and goats, brewed their own beer and made their own bread. It was his view that everybody should be as self-sufficient as possible, which would add to their own prosperity and contentment and to the eventual prosperity of the country.

William Cobbett was much concerned about the adulteration of bread in commercial bakeries and the price of the loaves in the shops and did all he could to promote home baking:

'How wasteful, then, and, indeed, how shameful, for a labourer's wife to go into a baker's shop; and how negligent, how criminally careless of the welfare of his family, must the labourer be, who permits so scandalous a use of the proceeds of his labour! ... As to the act of making bread, it would be shocking indeed, if that had to be taught by the means of books. Every woman, high or low, ought to know how to make bread.'

He nevertheless goes on to describe the bread-making process. 'And what is the result? Why, good, wholesome food, sufficient for a considerable family for a week, prepared in three or four hours.'

11

Folklore and Festival

*ALL OVER THE WORLD, BREAD IS SUCH A BASIC NECESSITY OF HUMAN LIFE THAT THERE
IS PROBABLY MORE FOLKLORE RELATED TO IT THAN TO ALMOST ANY OTHER FOOD.*

The many harvest customs that exist around the world date back to early times when corn was cut by hand.

The harvest festival is a service in which thanks are given for a good crop of corn, safely gathered in to provide food for the coming year.

The beginnings of ritual, tradition and religion are strongly linked to the baking of bread. Rituals and ceremonies developed to bring luck to the harvest and to ensure it was plentiful for the winter.

Harvest Festivals

Since wheat was first grown, about 9000 BC, a successful harvest has meant the culmination of a year's labour and the supply of a store of food for the months ahead – a time of celebration.

In pre-Christian times, the first day of the harvest was around 1 August, on the Celtic festival of Lughnasagh, the day of the sun god Lugh, and loaves baked on this day were offered to him in thanks. The day was later absorbed into the Christian tradition to become the Saxon *lafmass* ('loaf mass'); this later became the festival of Lammas, when loaves baked with wheat from the first harvest were taken to church to be blessed. In England in the 1980s, bakers introduced a Lammas loaf race, in which they competed to see who could cut the wheat, grind it and produce loaves in the shortest time.

Before the days of the combine harvester, Western European countries had many 'last load' customs. The last sheaf to be cut was thought to be where the corn spirit, who lived in the fields, had taken refuge. In some places, it was thought unlucky to be the person who cut the sheaf and so the harvesters threw their

sickles at it from a distance. In other places, it was the task of a young girl of the village to cut the sheaf, and she become the 'Harvest Queen'. The sheaf was garlanded with ribbons and flowers and taken back to the farm on a decorated cart, pulled by two horses, and the harvest was declared complete. In Sussex, England, the cry was:

> *We've ploughed,*
> *We've sowed,*
> *We've reaped,*
> *We've mowed,*
> *We've carried our last load*
> *And aren't overthrowed!*

Then it was back to the barn for the harvest supper where, in pride of place, there was a loaf baked in the shape of a wheatsheaf. This same wheatsheaf loaf is still baked for harvest celebrations in parts of Europe. It can be seen in bakers' shop windows and as part of church decorations for the harvest festival.

Bread Shapes

Almost every country has its own traditional shapes. Many of the shapes have origins and meanings that go back for many thousands of years. In Germany these breads are called *Gebiltbrote*, or 'picture breads'. Many shapes have pagan origins, while others have Christian significance. Both Germany and Switzerland have over 200 different bread shapes.

Plaited breads are made in many countries and it is said they go back to the time when widows sacrificed their hair following the death of a husband. In the same way, breads in the shape of farm animals replaced the yearly animal sacrifices to the gods.

Loaves in the shape of a sun, or marked with a star or wheel pattern, were used as sun symbols to honour the sun god at midsummer and Beltane (May Day). In some places they were rolled down hills, and in others placed at altars or ritually eaten. An equal-sided cross was added before it was used on hot-cross buns in Christian England during Lent or at Easter. The German pretzel was a moon symbol in honour of the moon goddess.

Bread plays a significant part in Eastern European weddings. This one is taking place in Russia.

A CALENDAR OF BREAD

The following celebrations can give only an idea of the extent to which bread plays a part in ritual and festival.

NEW YEAR

In one area of Switzerland, children who make lanterns for the New Year procession are given a small loaf called an *Altjahrman* ('old year man').

In the Ukraine, small sourdough rolls called *balabushky* are baked on New Year's Eve. One contains a coin and it is said that the girl who finds it will be married within the year.

In Greece, a New Year yeast cake, baked in a round tin and sprinkled with sesame seeds, is cut by the head of the family when the family members have all returned from church on New Year's Eve or New Year's morning.

TWELFTH NIGHT

In Spain, the three kings, *Los Reyes Majors*, arrive by camel from Bethlehem on the night of 6 January, bringing gifts and the *Roscon de Reyes*, or 'Three Kings' Cake', is baked. It is a rich yeast cake decorated with icing and candied peel, and often a trinket is baked inside, to bring good fortune to the person who receives it.

In Mexico, there is a *rosca de los reye*. The one to find the favour in the bread must give a party on 2 February.

Colomba

Around Easter time, in the Italian city of Milan, you can buy a rich, yeasted, almond cake shaped like a dove, known as colomba. *Milan being in Lombardy, where there are rich pasture lands, the dough for the cake is made with butter and eggs.*

The custom of making colomba goes back to the Easter of 1176, when the Milanese army was lined up with the rest of the forces of the Lombard League ready to fight for Pope Alexander III against the soldiers of the Holy Roman Empire. Two doves flew down and settled on the Milanese standards. The Milanese saw this as a symbol of divine protection. It encouraged them in the battle and they defeated the Emperor's army.

The anniversary of the battle is still commemorated in the Church of San Simpliciano in Milan, where a special mass is said and two doves are released from the altar.

Some harvest customs were designed not only to give thanks for the year's crop, but also to ensure plenty of corn, and therefore bread, in the year to come.

13

SHROVE TUESDAY AND ASH WEDNESDAY

Shrove Tuesday buns called *semlor* are baked in Sweden. They are small, round and sweet, filled with almond paste and served in a bowl of hot milk and cinnamon.

Still performed in Russia is a pre-Lent ceremony during which a young girl dressed as Spring is offered ceremonial bread and salt as a welcoming gift, while a man dressed as Winter receives a pitcher of wine as a farewell.

LENT

Apprentices of the Guild of Bakers in Switzerland finish their training in Lent by making *Lochli Brot* ('bread with holes').

In Turkey, Greece, Armenia and Cyprus, a rolled bread filled with olives was traditionally eaten during Lent to add flavour to a diet in which meat, eggs and dairy products were forbidden for 40 days.

PALM SUNDAY

In Mexico, Holy Week Bread, consisting of small rolls, is taken to church in a basket, together with medicinal herbs, local wine and sometimes money, as an offering to the poor.

GOOD FRIDAY

Small, sweet fruit buns with a cross on top, called hot cross buns, are baked in England on Good Friday. It was once believed that buns baked on that day would never go mouldy. They were nailed to the ceilings of houses and bakeries as a protection from fire. They were also kept to be used, crumbled into water, as a medicine for a number of ills.

In Russia, however, it was thought unlucky to bake on Good Friday and that if you did, the baked bread would turn into wood.

In Gundelmontag in Switzerland, a large loaf, with a head moulded on it, is impaled on a pole and taken round the town. Touching the head is supposed to bring good luck.

In Greece, the tsoureke, *a loaf baked with a coloured egg in the centre, is an esssential part of Easter celebrations.*

EASTER

In Estonia, Latvia and Lithuania *kulich*, a loaf made from rounds of spiced dough baked in a pyramid shape, is a key part of the Easter meal.

In Greece, the Lenten fast is ended with *tsoureke*, bread made from a rich dough coiled around a red-coloured hard-boiled egg.

HARVEST

One of the most spectacular of harvest festivals is the *Tabuleiros*, in Tomar in Portugal. Every year, 15 young girls are chosen to carry the *tabuleiro*, or 'tray', of bread in procession. The tray, in the form of a crown of bread rolls, is worn on the head and is often built up to be as tall as the wearer and decorated with sprigs of wheat and paper flowers. As each one weighs around 13kg (26lb), the girls are helped by male relatives. In the evening, oxen are killed and people are blessed at the Church of St John the Baptist. The next day there are bull fights, dancing and fireworks, and meat, wine and bread are given to the poor. The festival originated to honour the Roman goddess Ceres to offer thanks for a good and plentiful harvest, but is now a Christian celebration.

14

At the festival of Tabuleiros in Portugal, the young girls of the village of Tomar dress in white and wear crowns of bread. These girls are wearing the traditional costume of the area.

THE DAY OF THE DEAD (1 AND 2 NOVEMBER)
This festival, held to honour ancestors, takes place in Mexico. The special bread can be made in human, animal or plant shapes, or round and decorated with skulls, bones and tears of dough.

ST NICHOLAS' DAY (6 DECEMBER)
In Switzerland, various shaped breads, in the form of religious symbols and characters, are made for this day.

ST LUCIA'S DAY (13 DECEMBER)
This festival is celebrated in Sweden. Early in the morning, the daughter of the house is dressed in white, with a wreath of greenery and lighted candles on her head, to offer the rest of the household a plate of saffron buns. The buns are made in various animal shapes, but the most popular are the *lussekatter*, or cat's face.

Decorated gingerbread, in many different shapes, is popular at Christmas time in Germany.

CHRISTMAS
In Verona, Italy, *pan doro* (golden bread) is baked. It is rich with eggs and butter, baked in a star-shape and strewn with icing sugar.

Germany's main Christmas bread is *Dresdner stollen*, a rich fruit bread, packed with dried fruits, candied peel and flaked almonds, baked in a long shape and coated with icing sugar.

Scandinavian Christmas breads reflect the old Yule festivals that marked the winter solstice. Animal-shaped loaves, harking back to the old animal sacrifices, are still very popular. A Christmas bread made from Danish pastry dough, known as *Julekage*, is popular throughout the whole of Denmark.

Sweden has two Christmas breads. *Dopbrod* ('dipping bread'), made with rye flour and flavoured with fennel and anise seeds, is made both commercially and at home to dip into the Christmas Eve ham soup. *Prastens Har* ('priest's hair') made from white bread dough, is shaped like a wig with curls and decorated with dried and glacé fruits. Although the name and shape of the wig date from the seventeenth century, it is thought that the tradition is pre-Christian in origin.

15

In Mexico, the Day of the Dead festival is a time to honour and remember members of the family who have died. Candles are lit at dusk in their memory and special breads, decorated with skulls, bones and tears of dough, are baked.

BREAD AROUND THE WORLD

Every country has its own characteristic breads. Some breads are baked for festivals and for special occasions, but many are regional or national favourites that are baked every day. Some are served alongside other dishes, some are accompaniment and eating utensil in one, some are meals in themselves and others are sweet treats.

USA

Bread in the United States is the result of many influences, including Native American custom, frontier needs and the importation of ethnic specialities from different places of the world. A variety of corn breads (see pages 102–3) are still made, particularly in the south, and corn is also an ingredient in the steamed brown breads of New England, also often made with a mixture of flours. Early pioneers developed different sourdough bread recipes and salt rising breads that are still popular. In the north of the country and into Canada, bannocks, cooked over the fire in a flat pan, were food for trappers. Doughnuts came

Something tasty contained in bread always makes a hearty snack. The American hot dog (a bread roll containing a sausage) has become a popular snack worldwide

16

from the same area. In the east, more sophisticated types of bread were developed, such as Parker house rolls and Philadelphia sticky buns. Immigrants coming to America brought their own specialities. Jewish bagels, for example, came originally from Austria and the inspiration for muffins came from England.

CENTRAL AND SOUTH AMERICA

The grain indigenous to the countries in this area is maize, which is used to make the thin, flat breads called tortillas that are served with every meal in Mexico. Tortillas can also be deep-fried, either whole or in wedges, to make *tostadas* and *tostaditas*. The Spaniards introduced wheat to Mexico and it was soon adopted by the local people. South Americans like sweet things and many of the breads and rolls there contain a small amount of sugar.

THE WEST INDIES

Originating in the West Indies, cassava bread is still very popular today. It has an earthy flavour and can be eaten plain or fried. Maize is also indigenous to the area and corn breads are still popular. Wheat was taken to the West Indies by the first European settlers and today it is made into tin loaves, flat breads and rolls. Deep-fried pieces of plain dough called 'floats' are a favourite take-away snack in Trinidad. All over the West Indies there is a taste for sweet breads, containing ingredients such as bananas, limes, coconut, nuts and spices.

THE MIDDLE EAST

Wheat was first grown in the Middle East, where it has remained the staple grain used in hundreds of different breads. Widespread is *lavash*, a thin, slightly crisp bread that is baked in ovals and rounds in a clay oven called a *tonir*. Other flat breads include pitta bread from

In Mexico, tortillas are the staple bread, and many housewives still make them by hand in the traditional manner. The shaping and rolling process shown in this nineteenth-century print is still seen today.

Greece, *mannaeesh* from the Lebanon and *khobz-el-saluf* from the Yemen (both topped with herbs), and *barbari* from Iran. In Egypt, bread rings coated with sesame seeds are sold in the streets. Israel has bagels and also *cholla*, a rich, plaited bread made for the Jewish Sabbath.

SOUTH AFRICA
When the first Europeans arrived in South Africa, they had to devise ways of making bread without raising agents and without conventional ovens. They developed various sourdough breads and a salt rising bread very similar to the American ones. They also made small, hard rusks that would keep well on long journeys. *Mos*, made by fermenting raisins in water, was used as a starter for small, sweet buns. Bread was variously baked on a griddle or in a cast-iron pot and pieces of dough were deep fried to make *vetkoek* and *koeksisters* (see pages 118–19).

INDIA
Flatbreads are characteristic of India. The best known is chapati, made with a simple mixture of finely ground wholewheat flour, water and a little salt. A smaller, thicker variation is made from *gram* (chickpea) flour, often flavoured with coriander and chilli. There is also *roti*, made with chapati dough but cooked so that it puffs up. *Puris* are a deep-fried variation. More substantial and thicker again are *parathas*, which are enriched with *ghee*, a form of clarified butter.

CHINA
Although China is more often associated with rice or noodles, it still has some bread recipes, mainly from the north of the country. The dough is often steamed to keep it white and glossy. Most popular are the flower rolls, which are shaped by a sharp knife and a chopstick into elaborate spirals. Dim sum from Canton are steamed bun snacks with a sweet or savoury filling. The traditional accompaniment to Peking Duck is mandarin pancakes.

AUSTRALIA AND NEW ZEALAND
The first bread made by settlers in Australia was a round, unleavened loaf called a damper, baked in the ashes of a camp fire. It was originally made from plain flour and water, and extras such as salt and powdered milk were added when and if available. Today, health breads have come to the fore. The most popular recipes for home

baking are quick and easy, sweet tea-time treats.

Wheat was first grown in New Zealand in the early 1800s. It was quickly adopted by the Maori people, who devised a sourdough loaf, baked in a covered dish, called *rewena paraoa*. Nowadays, wholewheat and mixed grain breads are very popular in New Zealand.

GREAT BRITAIN
The breads of Great Britain range from simple, griddle-cooked oatcakes to rich, yeasted buns and cakes. The griddle, or girdle, was once common to the British household and on it were produced oatcakes and bannocks, Welsh cakes, Northumbrian singin' hinny, muffins, pikelets and crumpets. Most bread is made from wheat, and the most popular has always been white. Loaves are baked in different shapes, including

In the Middle East, freshly made flat breads, baked in a tandoor oven, can be bought in local outdoor markets.

Proverb from Afar

Better beans and corn bread at home than cake and wine in the land of strangers.

GEORGIAN SAYING. (GEORGIA WAS FORMERLY PART OF THE SOVIET UNION.)

the large, oval bloomer and tin loaves. Rich, sweet breads, such as the Scots black bun, West Country saffron cakes, *bara brith* from Wales and lardy cake (see page 74) are still popular. The speciality of Northern Ireland (and indeed of the Irish Republic) is soda bread, which is widely available in both white or wholewheat types.

FRANCE

The long, white baguette is the most recognisable of French breads but there are many others. Some are made with the same dough, differently shaped, and others are made with different flours or by using different methods. The French make superb rich breads. The Brioche (see page 58) is light and golden and can be made plain or filled, the flaky Croissant (see page 60) has become a favourite breakfast food in countries throughout the world.

GERMANY AND AUSTRIA

There are countless varieties of bread produced in hundreds of different shapes. Rye and wholewheat flours are popular, as are sourdough breads. These can be plain or flavoured with onion or caraway seeds. The everyday bread of Germany is *landbrot*. Usually made from rye

W̶ith a good supply of bread, the whole family will be kept well-fed and happy. A smiling housewife from Tuscany in Italy shows off her freshly baked loaves.

18

The Boulangerie

In France, very little bread is baked at home. There is a baker in every community and French housewives shop for bread daily.

The boulangerie, *or bread shop, is open even on a Sunday morning, and sometimes all day Sunday if it is combined with a* patisserie *(a section of the shop selling sweet pastries and cakes). Where there are several bakers in a community, they may well stagger their working hours to fit in with each other and to keep their customers supplied. A* boulangerie *is usually connected to a working bakery that produces fresh bread two or even three times a day.*

The proliferation of local bakers, rather than large, central bakeries producing sliced, wrapped loaves, ensures that a wide variety of bread is available throughout France. Besides the classic French baguette, boulangeries often sell up to 25 different types of bread, including regional specialities, many of which are peculiar to a small locality only. This turns shopping for bread in France into a culinary adventure

The Panetteria and the Forno

In Italy, every town or village has its own baker. In a large town or city it is referred to as a panetteria, *and in the smaller towns and villages as the* forno.

The panetteria *often has shelving and counters, and the windows display elaborate scenes of castles, farms or palaces all made from bread. It sells many different kinds of rich and speciality breads, such as focaccia, pizza,* panettoni *and even the French brioche.*

The forno *in a country village is often indistinguishable from an ordinary house. The whole process of baking and selling may take place in one room, or, if the building is larger, the oven may be situated in a room behind the shop. Loaves are baked several times a day and taken straight from the oven to the shop shelves. There is less variety than in the* panetteria *in the town, but the quality is always excellent.*

In the days when few, if any, of the village people had ovens in their own houses, pies, cakes and home-made breads were taken to the forno *for communal baking in the brick oven.*

flour, it has a dark, crispy crust and a light brown crumb. White flour is made into shaped breads and also into small, crusty rolls. Pretzels, made in twisted knot shapes, are a tasty snack.

Austria is justly famous for its rich, sweet breads such as *gugelhupf* (see page 62).

ITALY

There are many regional breads in Italy. In the northernmost region, hearty bread made from rye flour is eaten with main meals and soups, but wheat flour is used everywhere else. There are flatbreads, such as focaccia and pizza, and small, crispy breadsticks. The newest plain bread is the ciabatta, made with a long rising method to give a slightly sour flavour. Sweet specialities are *Panettoni* (see page 69), *Colomba* (see page 13) and the Christmas bread *pan doro*.

SCANDINAVIA

Throughout Scandinavia, rye is the most widely used grain for everyday breads and crispbreads which are made both with yeast and sourdough. Plain white bread is not frequently eaten and it is often referred to as 'French bread'. However, enriched white breads such as *pulla*, a plaited wreath made for Christmas, or the many versions of Danish pastry, are very popular.

The Galatea Tower in Figueres, Spain, has red walls decorated with bread.

19

SPAIN

Spanish bread is often baked in large loaves with a crisp crust and a soft crumb. White wheat flour is used throughout Spain and loaf shapes vary from region to region. In tapas bars you may find a bread snack called *la pringa*, made from small buns topped with a spiced pork filling. The New Year speciality is *Roscon de Reyes*.

FLOUR

The main ingredient of all breads is flour, which is produced by milling various types of grain. It comes in many different grades of coarseness and in colours ranging from pure white, through yellow, to dark brown. Although there is a wide variety of flours available, each country has its favourite.

Wholegrain flours contain the husk, endosperm and grain.

20

For centuries, water-mills and windmills have ground flour for the local community. Some, such as this one in St Céré, France, are still working.

TYPES OF GRAIN

Wheat is the grain most commonly used to make bread throughout the world. Rye has a stronger flavour and darker colour, and is very popular in certain European countries and in North America. Flours from oats and barley can also be made into bread, but are more often used in mixtures of different types of flour rather than alone. Maize or corn is used alone or in mixtures to make a variety of breads. The seeds of the buckwheat plant are also ground to make flour.

THE STRUCTURE OF GRAIN

A cereal grain is made up of three basic parts: the husk or bran, which makes up the outer coating; the endosperm, which makes up the bulk of the grain; and the germ, which is the small section at the base of the grain from which, if the grain were planted, the plant would grow. The husk has little nutritional value in terms of vitamins or minerals, but it can be an important source of dietary fibre. The endosperm makes up about 80 per cent of the grain and contains starch and proteins. The germ is rich in natural oil, iron, protein and vitamins B and E.

MILLING

Wholegrain flours are made by milling the husk, endosperm and germ together. For refined or white flours, all the husk and most of the germ are removed. There are also flours of varying degrees of coarseness with only a percentage of husk and germ removed. Stone-ground flour has been ground the old-fashioned way between millstones and many believe that it contains more vitamins and minerals than commercial flour which is slightly heated as it is ground.

TYPES OF FLOUR

Strong Plain Flour or 'Bread Flour' usually refers to white flour that has the bran and germ removed. It is the main bread-making flour.
Plain Flour is also referred to as soft plain flour. Although used mostly for cakes and pastries, it

is occasionally used for certain types of bread, including baguettes, flat breads such as *roti*, and quick breads made with baking powder or bicarbonate of soda. Bread dough made with plain flour absorbs less water than that made with strong flour. It is consequently less moist and will go stale more quickly.
All-purpose Flour is a white flour produced in the United States from a mixture of hard and soft wheats. It can be used for all types of bread and cakes and is easy to store.
Wholewheat Flour is the result of milling the whole of the wheat grain to produce a coarser textured, brown flour with higher levels of nutrients and fibre than white flour. It is also called wholemeal flour, but this term is more correctly used for any flour made from whole grains, whether wheat or another type. Wholewheat flour is available in both strong and plain varieties.
Brown Flour is wheat flour that retains a certain percentage of the germ and bran. It is sometimes sold as 85 per cent (or another percentage) flour, which refers to the proportion of the grain retained.
Sprouted Wheat Flour is a brown flour containing a certain amount of the germ and bran, plus whole wheat and rye grains that have been sprouted and toasted. It makes a nutty-flavoured, light loaf.

The McDougall's Flour Grader was a popular figure in the 1960s, made into promotional salt and pepper pots and flour sifters.

Flour of all types has been marketed under many different brand names. Some, such as Albatross, seem to bear no relation to the flour inside the packet.

Graham Flour was invented in the United States in the nineteenth century by a clergyman named Dr Sylvester Graham. It is a finely ground wholewheat flour.

Chapati Flour is a finely-ground wheat flour used in India for making flat breads. It is available in white and wholewheat varieties.

Cracked Wheat is not really a flour at all but coarsely broken wheat grains. It can be soaked or simmered in water and added to a dough to give a moist, dense texture (see Mixed Grain Bread, page 48), or used sprinkled dry over the tops of loaves before baking for a deocorative effect.

Semolina is made from a very hard wheat called durum wheat and consists of coarsely milled endosperm. It is more often used for pasta than for making bread.

Self-raising Flour is made from a soft wheat and is available in

Flour sifters, for the easy sprinkling of flour onto a worktop, have been made in many shapes and sizes.

both white and wholewheat varieties. Baking powder is added to the flour so that it is ready to use for making risen cakes and quick breads.

Rye Flour is often called rye meal. There are two types – dark and light. Dark rye flour contains the husk and germ of the grain as well as the endosperm. Light rye flour contains mostly endosperm, with small amounts of germ and husk. It is slightly coarser than a strong, plain wheat flour. When used alone, it is given a long rising time to prevent the bread becoming too heavy in texture. The sourdough method (see page 22) is particularly suitable.

Barley Flour is occasionally available from health food stores. To make a successful yeasted loaf it must be mixed with wheat flour. It can, however, be used for thin, flat breads and some unleavened breads.

Oat Flour and Oatmeal Oat flour is usually finely ground and makes a soft, moist loaf when mixed with wheat flour. Oatmeal consists of coarsely milled oat grain and is available in a variety of textures. Small amounts can be added to wheat flour to make a moist loaf with an interesting texture. Rolled oats can be used in the same way.

Buckwheat Flour Buckwheat is a seed rather than a grain. Bread made from buckwheat flour alone is very crumbly and does not rise well. It can be mixed with wheat or rye flours to make bread, and is often used in Eastern Europe and North America to make pancakes.

Maize Flours Cornmeal is produced by grinding the whole kernels of sweetcorn. To make yeasted or sourdough breads, it is often mixed with wheat flour. For quick breads, it can be used alone or in mixtures.

In Mexico, tortillas are made from a fresh pasta called *masa*. This is produced by first soaking corn kernels in a solution of lime so that they swell and the husks loosen, and then pounding and grinding them to a paste. For export, the *masa* is dried and broken up to produce *masa harina*, a coarse, yellow-brown flour.

Gram Flour is made in India from ground chickpeas and is used to make chapatis and other flat breads.

In this sixteenth-century woodcut, a farmer watches his sack of grain being poured into the hopper. This feeds the grain between the mill stones that will grind it into flour.

RAISING AGENTS

THE FIRST BREADS WERE SMALL, FLAT AND UNLEAVENED. ONCE THE TECHNIQUE OF FERMENTATION WAS DISCOVERED, LEAVENED BREADS BECAME POPULAR AND WERE SOON UNIVERSALLY PREFERRED. THE FIRST LEAVENED BREAD WAS A KIND OF SOURDOUGH. THEN YEAST CAME INTO USE, AND IN MORE RECENT YEARS, CHEMICAL RAISING AGENTS HAVE BEEN ADDED TO BREAD-MAKING INGREDIENTS.

Baking powder was invented in the nineteenth century and many brands with distinctive packaging and slogans have been produced over the years. This one proclaims itself 'double acting'.

SOURDOUGH STARTERS

Breads made with what has come to be called a 'sourdough' starter were the first leavened breads. Around 5000 BC, probably by chance, someone left a rather liquid flour-and-water mixture in a warm place only to discover, maybe a day later, that bubbles were forming on the surface and there was an interesting smell. As an experiment, more flour was added and the dough was baked, and the first risen loaf was produced, far superior in both flavour and texture to the hard, flat cakes that had been the staple diet of many people over the past 5000 years. It was soon found that, if a piece of this fermented dough was kept back, it could be mixed with a little more water and once again be put in a warm place, and the same process would take place. Bread mixtures ferment as a result of the natural yeasts that exist on the outside of every wheat grain, rather in the same way that wine can be made using only the natural yeasts on the skin of the grape.

Although yeast, a by-product of the brewing industry, was being used during Roman times, most bread in Europe was made by the sourdough method until the seventeenth century. A small amount of starter dough could be kept at all times, and a good quality bread could always be baked, whether an individual was nomadic or settled.

When the early Europeans went to North America, the sourdough technique went with them. Small amounts of starter were

San Francisco Sourdough

San Francisco Sourdough

125g • 4oz strong, plain flour
2tsp sugar
225ml • 8fl oz warm water

Put the flour and sugar into a bowl and stir in the water. Cover the bowl and leave it in a warm place for 2 days or until it is bubbling and risen. This is enough to make up a loaf using 750g/1½lb strong, plain flour.

Flour and Potato Starter

Flour and Potato Starter

1 medium potato
500g • 1lb 2oz strong, plain flour, wholewheat flour or rye flour
225g • 8oz sugar

Scrub the potato. Cut it in half, boil and drain it, reserving the water. Peel the potato and mash it in a large bowl. Make up the potato water to 850ml/30fl oz with more warm water. Stir it into the mashed potato. Stir in the flour and sugar. Cover the bowl with plastic film and leave it in a warm place for about 3 days or until it is bubbling and smells sour.
Once it is at this stage, your starter will be alive. It can be used immediately or you can stir in another 60g/2oz flour and 150ml/5fl oz warm water to keep it going.
To make a loaf using this starter, put three-quarters of the mixture into a bowl and stir in enough flour to make a dough of a kneadable consistency. Let the dough rise and bake it as normal.
Into the remaining quarter of starter, stir 350g/12oz flour, 30g/1oz sugar and 600ml/1pt warm water. Cover the bowl and return it to its warm place.

carried west on wagon trains, and on the Canadian borders, lone trappers became known as 'sourdoughs', because they were never without the means of making a nutritious loaf.

Although yeast is now the main raising agent used for bread, there are many countries in which sourdough loaves have remained firm favourites, notably Eastern Europe, France, Germany and the United States. Ciabatta, a new loaf from Italy, is made with a long rising time to give it a sourdough flavour.

Sourdough bread has a rich flavour and moist texture, and once the starter is made you will never have to worry about whether or not you have any yeast. A starter will take a few days to become active, but after the first batch it is a simple matter to keep several batches on hand at various stages of development.

YEAST

In the seventeenth century, a leaven made from brewer's yeast was made popular by the Flemish, and its use gradually spread, but because there was no standard baker's yeast available, bread-making could be a hit and miss affair, regardless of the cook's skill.

In the nineteenth century, the famous scientist Louis Pasteur discovered that yeast is a living plant composed of a single cell. His research led to a reliable baker's yeast becoming commercially available. The species that is now used to make baker's yeast is *Saccharomyces cerevisiae* which, when it is cultivated in warm, humid surroundings, reproduces itself rapidly.

Various types of yeast are available to the home baker today, and everyone has their own preferences.

Fresh Yeast Fresh yeast can be stored in greaseproof paper, placed in a plastic bag and put into the refrigerator, where it will keep for up to two weeks. If you rarely get the opportunity to buy fresh yeast, you can buy a large block and freeze it in small portions, again wrapped in greaseproof and plastic film. Yeast can be used frozen, but it needs to be sprinkled into warm water and left for about 30 minutes before the dough is mixed.

Recipes vary as to the amount of fresh yeast needed, but it is usually 15–30g/½–1oz per 450–500g/1lb–1lb 2oz flour.

When using fresh yeast, place a little warm water in a bowl (see individual recipes for amounts) and crumble the required amount of yeast into it. Leave for 5 minutes in a warm place so that the liquid begins to bubble. Then use as the recipe directs.

Fresh yeast should be firm and moist, with a fresh scent, and should crumble easily between your fingers. Buy it by the gram or ounce.

Dried Yeast Dried yeast comes in conveniently sized pots or sachets, which can be stored unopened for up to six months.

When baking, use half the weight of dried yeast that that you would use of fresh. To use,

put the amount of warm water specified for your recipe into a bowl. Sprinkle the yeast on top and leave in a warm place for 15 minutes or until the liquid begins to bubble. If you find that the particular brand of yeast you are using is slow to start fermenting, next time add 1tsp sugar to the water before sprinkling the yeast on top. If you are using a brand of yeast that you have not used before, it is worth experimenting first to find out how long it takes to ferment.

Easy-bake Yeast is a dried yeast generally available in measured sachets. It can usually be added dry to the flour without fermenting first in water. Easy-bake yeast can be substituted for fresh or dried yeast in all the recipes in this book.

CHEMICAL RAISING AGENTS

Chemical raising agents are easy to use, and raised loaves and cakes can be mixed and in the oven in minutes. This is because, although chemical raising agents begin to take effect in the dough when liquid is added, they become more active when the dough is in the oven. The main drawback of bread made with chemical raising agents is that it is not as moist as yeast or sourdough bread and so is best eaten almost as soon as it comes out of the oven, and certainly on the day it is baked.

Bicarbonate of Soda is an alkaline raising agent. Like yeast, it releases carbon dioxide when moistened and heated.

When bicarbonate of soda is used alone, it can give a 'soapy' alkaline flavour to bread. In some recipes, such as soda bread and scones, this is neutralised by the addition of an acid ingredient such as soured milk, cultured buttermilk or natural yoghurt. Alternatively, some recipes suggest the use of a little cream of tartar, which has the same effect.

Baking Powder is a mixture of bicarbonate of soda and cream of tartar to which a small amount of starch, usually cornflour, has been added to act as an anti-caking agent.

Dried yeast is often supplied in individual sachets, each holding enough to make one large loaf.

Baking powder and bicarbonate of soda come in the form of fine, white powders that are mixed with the flour before any liquid is added.

23

ADDED INGREDIENTS

THE ESSENTIAL INGREDIENTS OF BREAD ARE FLOUR, A RAISING AGENT AND A LIQUID. BUT THERE IS NO NEED TO STOP THERE. MANY OTHER INGREDIENTS ARE OFTEN ADDED TO ALTER THE FLAVOUR AND TEXTURE OF BREAD, RESULTING IN THE VAST RANGE OF DIFFERENT BREADS THAT EXISTS AROUND THE WORLD.

SALT

Salt is not just an extra ingredient. It is essential in most bread recipes, even sweet ones. Bread baked without salt has a strange, bland, sweetish flavour. Even a small amount of salt will counteract this. On average, for a plain loaf, 2tsp salt are added for every 450–500g/1lb–1lb 2oz flour.

Fine salt can be added to the flour before the yeast-and-water mixture is stirred in. Coarse salt should be dissolved in a little of the water before it is added so that it is evenly distributed. Do not, however, dissolve it in the same water that you are using to start off the yeast. Salt will inhibit the action of the yeast, and so they should not come into contact until the yeast has at least begun to ferment. In recipes where a 'sponge' is made with the yeast and some of the given amount of flour to act as a starter for the dough, the salt should be added to the second batch of flour.

LIQUIDS

Water is the main liquid used for most types of bread dough. However, some or all of it can be replaced. All liquids should be heated to lukewarm before they are added.

Milk is the most popular substitute for water. A milk loaf will have a soft crumb and a thinner crust than bread made with water. It may, however, become dry and stale more quickly than an ordinary loaf. When milk is the main liquid in soda bread, it should have a little cream of tartar added to counteract the alkalinity of the soda.

Fermented Milk Products, such as plain yoghurt, cultured buttermilk or ordinary soured milk, produce a rich flavour and a soft texture in a yeasted loaf. For quick breads made with bicarbonate of soda as a raising agent, they are essential in order to counteract the alkalinity of the soda.

Cream and Soured Cream Cream gives a rich texture to yeasted loaves. When making scones or soda bread, use soured cream for the same effect.

Vegetable Juices When you are making a loaf to go with savoury foods such as soups and salads, a tomato or mixed vegetable juice used instead of water will give a delicious, savoury flavour and an orange colour. Carrot juice tends to be too sweet for savoury breads, but it can be used when making tea breads, such as the Carrot Tea Bread (see page 109).

Fruit Juices can be added to enrich sweet breads, particularly those containing dried fruits. They are suitable for both yeasted breads and tea breads. In yeasted breads they give a mild, sweet flavour and a subtle colour. Pure orange juice is the most suitable.

Beer can be used to make strongly flavoured breads with wholegrain flours. It gives a distinctive, slightly bitter flavour. Beer can also be used instead of water to make a sourdough starter.

Eggs will enrich and soften all yeasted breads and are best used in combination with other enriching ingredients, such as milk, butter or olive oil. If used to replace all or part of the liquid in a recipe, they may produce a loaf that becomes

dry-textured after 24 hours. When you are replacing a liquid in a recipe with eggs, take into account their liquid measurement. The best way to ascertain this is to beat them in a measuring jug.

FATS AND OILS
Butter will give a moist, flaky texture to dough and, if used in large quantities, a golden colour. Unless otherwise stated, salted butter is used for bread-making.

Margarine will enrich a bread dough but will not give as good a flavour as butter. Use it only when small amounts are required, either for yeasted bread or for quick breads.

Butter Substitutes and Spreads These are not suitable for bread-making.

Lard is a soft, white fat made from rendered animal fat. It was used in traditional recipes such as Lardy Cake (see page 74) but is rarely used nowadays. Lard is very rich and people mostly prefer to use butter instead.

Shortening is a soft, white vegetable fat with a similar texture to lard. It is rarely used for yeasted breads but is sometimes called for in American Muffins (see page 99) and in some tea bread recipes.

Olive Oil enriches, softens and flavours many of the breads of the world, particularly those from Spain, Italy and France. Often it is added with the liquid, in which case the amount of liquid that you use may have to be reduced slightly. Other recipes call for the olive oil to be kneaded into the dough. This may sometimes appear to be an impossible task, but if the oil is added in 1 or 2 tbs at a time and care is taken to knead it all in before adding the next spoonful, you will find that it can be gradually incorporated.

Sunflower Oil will enrich a bread dough in a similar way to olive oil but will not give a very good flavour. It can, however, be used as a butter or lard substitute in certain tea breads.

Sesame Oil will give a rich, nutty flavour to a loaf. It can replace olive oil but should be used only in small quantities in appropriate recipes, such as Middle Eastern breads.

SWEETENERS
Sweeteners can be added to bread doughs in varying amounts. They may make the loaf very dark on the outside. This does not mean that the bread is burned.

Granulated Sugar is used in a wide range of bread recipes. It is essential if you want to produce a white-coloured crumb and can be added to the flour with the salt or dissolved in the liquid before it is added.

Caster Sugar Caster sugar is not necessary for most bread recipes, but it may be specified for some particular types, such as tea breads.

Brown Sugar will add colour and a small amount of flavour to a loaf. It is often used in combination with a wholegrain flour where it is not necessary to preserve a white colour.

Honey can be used for tea breads and muffins. It makes a sticky, yeasted dough and so is rarely used for yeast breads in large quantities.

Molasses Small amounts of molasses make interesting yeast breads and tea breads (see Steamed Brown Bread, page 106).

FLAVOURINGS
For even more variety, different flavourings can be added to loaves, and in many cases only small amounts are needed. Both fresh and dried herbs can be added to savoury loaves. Spices added in fairly small quantities give flavour to both sweet and savoury loaves. Black olives, sundried tomatoes, tomato paste and garlic paste all add flavour to the dough. Mashed potato makes a soft, moist bread. Dried fruits, glacé cherries, candied peel, and chopped nuts are popular choices for enriched yeast breads.

25

Equipment

Most of the equipment required for successful bread-making can readily be found in the kitchen. If you regularly make bread, you may want to use one or two more specialist items to make your work easier and improve the appearance of your loaves.

Work Surface

A clear work surface is essential for making bread. If your kitchen worktops are smooth and clean, you can use them. If you have tiles or a rough-surfaced area, it is best to use some kind of board or slab on which to knead your dough. Keep it specifically for that purpose. A large marble slab is ideal. So, too, is a large plastic chopping board, as long as it has not been grooved by frequent cutting with sharp knives, or a large wooden board covered with a laminated layer. Always take care to thoroughly clean and dry your work surface after use, so that it is ready for next time.

Scales

An accurate pair of scales will ensure that you use the right amounts of flour and other ingredients.

Measuring Jugs

Several measuring jugs of different sizes are useful. If you have a microwave oven, use microwave-safe jugs so that you can warm or melt ingedients in them.

Bowls

Large mixing bowls are essential for making bread. They should be big enough to allow you to knead the dough in the bowl, if necessary, and to allow the kneaded dough to rise without overflowing the bowl.

Small mixing bowls are useful for starting off yeast, beating eggs and mixing small amounts of flavouring ingredients.

If you have a microwave oven, use microwave-safe bowls so that you can warm and melt ingredients.

Microwave

This is not essential but is an easy way of warming and melting ingredients and saves washing up saucepans.

Measuring Spoons

These are useful for measuring out salt and small amounts of other ingredients such as spices and herbs. Absolute accuracy is not essential with these ingredients but using standard measuring spoons will help you to get the same good results each time you use a recipe.

Cutlery

Both round-bladed knives and tablespoons are useful for mixing dough. Use forks for beating eggs.

Wooden Spoons

Moist doughs and batter-type mixes are best prepared with a wooden spoon.

Dough Scraper

Although not essential, this is a useful utensil if you bake bread often. It is a plastic, rectangular, pliable scraper used for scraping dough from bowls and off work surfaces.

CLOTHS

Use clean linen tea towels to cover bowls of rising dough. Keep them separate from other kitchen cloths, wash after every use and use them only for bread-making.

BREAD TINS

Regular bread tins come in two basic sizes: 500g/1lb 2oz and 1kg/2lbs 4oz. A 500g/1lb 2oz tin will hold dough made with around 225g/8oz flour. A 1kg/2lbs 4oz bread tin will hold dough made with around 500g/1lb flour. This allows for the dough to double in size while it is proving and baking.

Specialist bread recipes will call for other types of tins. Flat breads can be baked in shallow, rectangular or square tins. Some loaves are made in round tins. Brioche moulds are fluted and come in a variety of sizes for making loaves ranging from bun-sized to 500g/1lb 2oz. *Gugelhupf* moulds are also fluted but larger and ring-shaped.

All these are available with standard or non-stick surfaces. All should be oiled lightly with sunflower or a similar oil before the first use. After this, non-stick tins may not need further oiling, but follow the manufacturer's instructions.

BAKING TRAYS

Both non-stick and uncoated surfaces are available. Follow the manufacturer's instructions before use. Although some recipes call for baking trays to be oiled, this makes them very hard to clean and is rarely necessary. A dusting of flour will make life much easier. If it is essential to put bread on an oiled surface, cover your trays with aluminium foil and oil the foil. The foil can then be thrown away after use and your tray will be clean.

BRUSHES

Small, soft pastry brushes are used for oiling bread tins and also for brushing the surface of loaves with a glazing agent, such as beaten egg or oil, before baking.

ROLLING PIN

Some recipes require the dough to be rolled into a certain shape before baking or rolled out thinly before being covered with other ingredients, folded and shaped. Use a long, straight, wooden rolling pin.

ELECTRIC MIXERS

An electric mixer with a dough hook will successfully mix bread dough. However, the baker's skill lies in being able to judge the correct consistency of the dough by its feel. It is also very therapeutic to make bread by hand. Whether you use an electric mixer is a matter of personal choice.

BREAD-MAKING MACHINES

A bread-making machine takes all the work out of making bread. You put in the ingredients, set the controls, walk away, and a perfect loaf is ready at the time of your choosing. It is an excellent way to make fresh bread to order without having to put in any effort. Most bread machines come with a variety of cycles designed to handle speciality breads or to prepare the dough for hand-shaped breads and rolls.

TYPES OF BREAD

BREAD COMES IN ALL SHAPES AND SIZES, AND IN MANY DIFFERENT TEXTURES, COLOURS AND FLAVOURS. USING JUST ONE SIMPLE, BASIC MIXTURE, THE POSSIBILITIES ARE ENDLESS.

PLAIN BREADS

The basic loaf is made from flour, a raising agent, salt and water. It has a flavour that will complement sweet or savoury dishes, and it can be sliced, cubed or crumbled to form the basis of many meals.

Yet, within that definition, bread can take many different forms. With only a slight variation of the mixing or baking method, or even a change of shape, the flavour and texture can be altered. The type of yeast or other raising agent that you use also makes a difference.

A plain bread dough can be made into loaves and rolls of many different shapes and sizes.

Plain loaves can be made from one type of flour or a mixture, allowing endless combinations and variations. They can be mixed with fresh yeast, dried yeast or easy-bake yeast. Fresh yeast, in some cases, gives a more risen, lighter texture, whereas dried yeast often produces a close texture.

With plain breads, you can make small changes and additions to the ingredients without fundamentally changing their character. Milk can be used instead of water, butter can be rubbed into the flour or oil added with the liquids. A little added sugar produces sweeter breads, such as *Peineta* (see page 51) or *Massa Sovada* (see page 49).

A longer rising time than the usual one hour, such as that needed to make Ciabatta (see page 53) or Fannie Farmer's Water Bread (see page 43), results in a richer flavour. The sourdough method produces a richer flavour again.

The final shape of a loaf also changes its texture. A flat bread, for example, has more of its surface exposed to the heat and so has more crust. Some breads baked on a baking tray have a slightly drier texture than those baked in a tin. When dough is formed into rolls, there is even less crumb in relation to crust and this is why rolls do not keep well.

Most breads are baked in a dry oven. Some, recipes, however, require a pan of water to be placed in the bottom of the oven so that the surface of the dough can be steamed, which softens the crust. A Baguette (see page 51) needs to be brushed with water to produce a crisp, crackling crust. Bagels (see page 52) are briefly immersed in boiling water before being baked, which makes the outside smooth and shiny. Other breads, such as English Muffins (see page 40), are baked on a griddle, giving them a moist texture and a thin, crisp outside.

ENRICHED BREADS

The main ingredients of enriched breads are similarly flour, a raising agent, salt and water, but larger proportions of other ingredients are added to change the flavour and texture.

Enriched breads can be made from a basic bread dough, with the addition of flavouring ingredients, such as dried fruits or olives (see page 25). A plain dough can also be used as a base for an open tart that is to be filled with a rich sweet or savoury filling, or it can form an outside wrapping for a savoury filling, as in Prawn and Beanshoot Buns (see page 70). Enriching ingredients, such as butter, milk and eggs, are often mixed into bread dough. The Sally Lunn (see page 62) and Brioche (see page 58) recipes are good examples of this. For some breads, enriching ingredients need to be added in a special way

Bread dough can be enriched with butter, eggs or milk, or other ingredients – such as chopped meats or nuts, or dried fruits – which can be kneaded in.

Thomas Muffett's Advice on Bread-making

'Things to be observed in the well-making of Bread — whereof we must have great choice and care:

1. of the Weate itself *6. of the Dough or Paste*
2. of the Meal *7. of the Moulding*
3. of the Water *8. of the Oven*
4. of the Salt *9. of the Baking*
5. of the Leaven

All which circumstances I most willingly prosecute to the full, because as Bread is the best nourishment of all other, being well-made; so it is simply the worst being marred in the ill handling.'

Thomas Muffett (1553–1604) *was a physician, a medical and scientific writer, and a poet, whose patients included members of the court of Queen Elizabeth I. Fifty years after his death, his daughter, Patience, organised the publication of his book,* Health's Improvement, *which was originally written in 1595.*

and sometimes both enriching ingredients and flavouring ingredients are added.

FLAT BREADS

Flat breads are variously made from yeasted, unleavened and chemically-raised dough. They can be baked in the oven or on a griddle, either plain or with a topping.

The first breads were made from unleavened dough, rolled into small rounds and baked on a hot stone, and this type of bread is still enjoyed today in many parts of the world. Indian Chapatis (see page 84) and Mexican Tortillas (see page 88) are thin and pliable and serve both as an eating utensil and an accompaniment to spicy foods. *Parathas* are slightly thicker and eaten as an accompaniment. *Knackebrod* (see page 86) and Danish Crispbreads (see page 81), both from Scandinavia, are crisp and best eaten with cheese.

Yeasted flat breads should be baked until they are just cooked through, so that even with their large surface area they are still soft enough to bend and to dip into other food. They are popular in the Middle East, where many different types can be found at roadside markets and stalls. Pitta Bread (see page 88) is baked on heated trays and a pocket is formed into which food can be stuffed.

The Italian pizza forms a base for a savoury topping and the same dough is folded round cheese or ham to make the rich snack known as Calzone (see pages 82-3).

Focaccia, slightly thicker but still soft in texture, can be made plain or can be topped with a variety of ingredients, from simple salt and chopped sage to a mixture of sliced vegetables.

British flat breads are often baked on a griddle, and the Germans and Austrians like to give flat breads a sweet topping and eat them with morning coffee or afternoon tea.

QUICK BREADS

The term 'quick bread' usually refers to the fact that the dough has been mixed quickly without having to undergo a long rising time. It does not necessarily mean that the bread also cooks quickly.

Plain and flavoured soda breads are usually quick to mix and quick to make. The same basic mixture can be cut into rounds to make scones, and it can be baked in the oven or on a griddle. *Roti* (see page 104) is a Caribbean, griddle-baked soda bread served with curries. American Muffins (see page 99) are also a type of quick bread, even though they are more often regarded as cake.

Tea breads are a cross between bread and cake. They are generally too sweet and light-textured to be called 'bread' but they are not as rich and light as a true cake. They are served sliced and sometimes buttered as a mid-afternoon snack.

Flat bread can be baked in any size, but it is rarely more than 4cm/ 1½ in thick.

BASIC TECHNIQUES

THE BASIC TECHNIQUES OF BREAD-MAKING APPLY TO ALL TYPES OF BREAD. IT IS BEST TO BEGIN BY LEARNING HOW TO MAKE A PLAIN LOAF. ONCE YOU HAVE MASTERED THIS YOU CAN EASILY PROGRESS TO ADDING EXTRA INGREDIENTS OR MAKING A PARTICULAR SHAPE OF LOAF.

STEP-BY-STEP GUIDE TO MAKING A BASIC LOAF

MAKES ONE 1KG/2LB 4OZ LOAF

30g • 1oz fresh yeast or 15g •   *500g • 1lb 2oz strong plain*
½oz dried yeast   *flour*
300ml • 10fl oz warm water   *2tsp salt*

Note: The quantity of water given here is the average quantity for the amount of flour. However, some types of flour, such as wholewheat, can absorb more water, and so you may have to add a little extra to the bowl if the mixture feels particularly dry. It is better to err on the wet side rather than the dry, since it is easier to knead in more flour on the work surface than it is to add more water.

The amount of flour given in a recipe is the amount needed to make that particular loaf. It does not take into account the small extra amount that you will always need to flour your hands and the work surface before kneading the bread. Always have extra flour on hand for this purpose.

STARTING THE YEAST

Put half the water into a small bowl and sprinkle in all the yeast. Leave the yeast in a warm place, allowing 5 minutes for fresh yeast and 15 minutes for dried yeast. When the yeast has started to work, you will see small bubbles appearing in the liquid. The liquid does not have to be particularly frothy; one or two small bubbles are all you need. On warm days, yeast will begin to work quite quickly. On very cold days, the process may take a little longer. You can speed it up by placing the bowl by a warm radiator or on top of a stove when the oven is turned on.

MIXING

Put the given amount of flour into a large mixing bowl. If you are using fine salt, toss it into the flour with your fingertips. If you are using coarse salt, dissolve it in the remaining water.

Make a well in the centre of the flour. Pour in all the yeast-and-water mixture and, using a round-bladed knife, mix in a little flour from the edges of the

well. Pour in the remaining water and begin to mix in the rest of the flour from the edges. Once the flour and water have been roughly mixed, begin using your hands to turn the flour until the water is incorporated and you have a lumpy, uneven dough. If the dough feels very stiff, mix in a little more water, 1tbsp at a time. If it feels very wet, work in a little more flour. These extra amounts will not inhibit the rising of the dough, and if you take care at this stage, you will find that kneading will be easier and the baked bread will have perfect texture.

KNEADING

Sprinkle flour over a clean work surface. Tip the dough out of the bowl onto the work surface, using your hands or a dough scraper to remove it all from the sides of the bowl. Rub off any dough that may have stuck to your hands and then coat your hands with a little flour. Gather the dough into one lump. To knead the dough, first push it slightly away from you using the palms of both hands and then pull it back towards you with your fingertips. Continue to push and pull in this way, using a constant, rhythmic action. After about ten times you will find that the dough has become elongated, so fold in both ends, give the dough a quarter turn and repeat the process. After approximately three minutes you will find that the texture of the dough has started to become smoother.

Kneading also forces out any air pockets that may have developed in the dough, which would cause it to rise unevenly. Continue kneading for 5–7 minutes. Then fold in the ends of the dough for the last time. Place the dough on the work surface with the

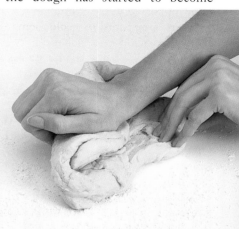

ends tucked underneath and rotate it to make it into a smooth, round ball. Return it to the bowl. Cut a cross in the top with a sharp knife to help it to rise easily. Unless otherwise stated in the recipe, cover the bowl with a clean, dry cloth.

KNEADING IN THE BOWL

Some recipes, such as that for Ciabatta (see page 53), call for the dough to be much moister than for a standard loaf. Wet mixtures like this are always kneaded in the bowl. To do this, first flour your hands. Using your right hand, keep taking the sides of the dough to the middle as your left hand rotates the bowl in a clockwise direction. (If you are left-handed, knead with your left hand and rotate the bowl in an anti-clockwise direction with your right.) Even when the dough is wet, you will still be able to detect changes in texture. If the dough is dry enough, make a cross-cut in the top. If the dough is more like a thick batter, there is no need to do this. Cover the bowl with a clean, dry cloth.

RISING

Put the bowl in a warm place away from draughts. The yeast will now begin the fermentation process that makes the dough rise. It needs to double in size. This usually takes an hour. However, in warm summer weather the dough could be ready in 30 minutes. In a cold room in winter, it may need 1½ hours. You will also find that different types of dough rise at different rates. Often, the richer the loaf, the longer it takes to rise.

SECOND KNEADING

When the dough has risen sufficiently, return the bowl to the work surface. Punch the dough down with the back of your hand and then turn it onto the work surface. Knead it in the same way as before, pushing out any air pockets. This second kneading should take about three minutes. At this stage the dough should be very smooth, and you will need only a sprinkling of flour on the work surface and on your hands. The dough is now ready to be shaped and finished (see Bread Shapes and Finishes, page 32).

PROVING

Once the loaf has been shaped, it will need to stand in a warm place for a second, shorter rising. This takes only 15–20 minutes and is called 'proving'. Some doughs will double in size during this time; others, particularly the richer breads, will rise only a little but will rise considerably during baking.

BAKING

Whatever type of bread you are baking, the oven should be preheated, so turn it on halfway through the first rising time to make sure it is up to temperature when you need it. Most breads are baked at 200°C/400°F/gas mark 6, but follow the instructions given in the recipe.

Before moving your loaves from where they are proving to the oven, make sure that your oven racks are in the right position and that there is sufficient room above each loaf for it to rise freely. Open the oven door and transfer the loaves quickly and smoothly to their place in the oven.

A 1kg/2lb 4oz loaf will take 35–40 minutes to bake in a standard oven. If you have a fan-assisted oven it will take only 30 minutes, so check at this time to see if the loaf is done. A cooked loaf will be golden brown on the outside and will sound hollow when tapped.

COOLING

Have a cooling rack ready. Take the loaf out of the oven and immediately turn it out of the loaf tin or baking container, or lift it from the baking tray. Loaves that stay in hot tins may continue to cook for a little longer than is needed, and as they cool down, they sweat inside the tin, producing a damp crust. Loaves baked on a baking tray will develop a thick, damp undercrust if they are left on the tray to cool.

Place the loaf on the cooling rack and leave it until it is cold before serving. Bread eaten straight from the oven is still moist and steamy inside and has a doughy texture, and once the crust has gone, the cut side will dry out. So resist the temptation – and let the loaf cool!

BREAD SHAPES AND FINISHES

BREAD DOUGH CAN BE FORMED INTO MANY DIFFERENT SHAPES. IT SHOULD NEVER BE STRETCHED, BUT SHOULD BE EASED INTO SHAPE GRADUALLY SO THAT IT WILL NOT SPRING BACK WHEN BAKED.

BAKING CONTAINERS
Standard Bread Tin The amount of dough made in the recipe given for the basic loaf will fit into a 1kg/2lb 4oz loaf tin. Oil your tin lightly before you start to shape the loaf. After the last kneading, fold the sides of the dough into the middle and then, with your left hand on top of your right hand, press the dough out flat to a thickness of about 4cm/1 ½in so that it forms a rectangle about the same length as the loaf tin. Roll it up from one long side. Put the roll of dough into the tin with the end of the roll on the underside. Gently push the dough down several times with the back of your fist.

32

When dough has been sufficiently kneaded, it should feel smooth and not sticky. It is now ready to be shaped.

Round Containers Bread can be baked in round containers of various sizes. You can use a round cake tin or a French charlotte tin to make round loaves. A spring-form 5cm/2in high tin will make a loaf with an even-shaped base but a top that can rise both upwards and sideways. To shape a round loaf, fold the edges of the dough from the sides to the middle after the first kneading. Turn the loaf over so that the edges are tucked underneath. Then rotate the loaf, tucking under the sides as you do so, to make a round, dome shape.

Cylindrical Loaves Cylindrical hinged moulds are available that completely enclose the dough so that it rises to fit the mould. Baking a loaf completely enclosed in this way produces a thin crust and a very even crumb.

Rectangular or Square Tins Some flat breads are baked in square or rectangular cake tins, usually about 5cm/2in deep.

Special Containers
Breads such as French Brioche and Austrian *Kugelhupf* are baked in specially shaped containers, which can also be used for plainer breads.

Ring Mould To make a ring of bread, shape the dough into a long, tapered cylinder. Coil it round inside the mould, over-lapping the tapered ends so that the join forms the same thickness as the rest of the loaf.

Flower Pot Loaves baked in a flower pot were once popular. Use a new, earthenware flower pot and leave it in a warm place for 24 hours to dry out. Oil it well with sunflower oil and put it into a preheated oven at 200°C/400°F/gas mark 6 for 45 minutes. When completely cool, it can be used in the same way as a bread tin. Never wash a flower pot once it has been seasoned. Wipe it with paper towels after use.

Bread Pots Special earthenware bread pots, similar to a flower pot but often wider, are available from cookware shops. Prepare them in the same way as a flower pot.

SHAPING LOAVES FOR A BAKING TRAY

Round Loaves A round loaf to be baked on a tray is shaped in the same way as for a round tin.

Cottage Loaf Divide the dough into two pieces of about one-third and two-thirds. Make each into a round shape and flatten both slightly. Place the smaller one on top of the larger one and press down evenly. Using the handle of a wooden spoon, make a hole right down through the centre of both pieces of dough. This gives the loaf shape and is also a way of ensuring that both pieces of dough stay together.

Square Cottage Divide the dough into two pieces as for a cottage loaf. Form each piece into a square shape and place the smaller one on top of the larger. Using the side of your flat hand, make a slit-shaped hole right through both pieces of dough from top to bottom.

Spiral Make a long cylinder of dough. Coil it round from the centre outwards to form a spiral.

Cylinder Make a round of dough and leave it on the work surface to rest for a few minutes. Flatten the dough with your hands to a thickness of about 2.5cm/1in. Roll up the dough and then roll it backwards and forwards under your hands, working from the centre outwards, to make a long, even shape. Flatten the dough out again into a rectangle. Fold both ends to the centre and press down hard. This ensures an even shape. Roll up the dough tightly from one long side to make an evenly shaped cylinder.

Ring Make a round loaf. Push the handle of a wooden spoon down through the centre. Put two fingers into the hole made by the spoon and gradually work them round. With your fingers inside the hole and the palms of your hands on

To make a ring shape, first push the handle of a wooden spoon through the dough and then enlarge the hole with your fingers.

the edge of the ring, gradually ease out the dough to make the hole about 15cm/6in in diameter. You will have to stretch it, so do it slowly and let the dough rest several times during the process.

BREAD SHAPES MADE BY SLASHING DOUGH

Slashing the surface of the dough with a sharp knife will make the loaf shape more interesting, as well as creating more surface area and therefore more crust. Various patterns can be made using long slashes down the centre, short diagonal slashes across the length of a loaf or even a chequerboard pattern on the surface of a large round loaf. Some loaves take their shape and name from the type of slash commonly used when making them. Most slashes are made after proving.

Crown Shape the dough into a round and stand it on a baking tray. Score a circle in the top about 2.5cm/1in in from the edges. The centre part will then rise above the rest.

MAKING A PLAIT

Divide the dough into three equal parts. Roll each piece underneath your hands, working from the centre outwards, to make a long, thin cylinder. Begin the plait from the centre outwards to make a more even shape.

Complete one half first and, as you near the end, stretch the tips slightly and push them downwards towards the surface to shape and seal the ends. Form the other half of the plait in the same way.

As it bakes, the plait should expand evenly to form a shape resembling an ear of wheat, as shown above.

The Coburg loaf is formed by making a flat round and then cutting a cross in the top. The corners of the dough formed by the cross will rise slightly higher than the rest of the loaf.

Coburg This is a round loaf shaped by making a cross-cut in the top. Make one long cut down the centre, scoring the top of the loaf in half. Make the second cross-cut in two halves, working from the centre outwards.

Chequerboard Make a round loaf. Score three parallel lines across the top and three more running at right angles.

Miche Make a round loaf and score the top into six sections. First make one long slash down the centre of the loaf, not quite to the edges. Make the other slashes from the centre of the first slash outwards, again not quite to the edges of the loaf.

Bloomer Make a cylindrical loaf and gently point the ends. Make diagonal slashes across the top about 4cm/1½in apart.

Vienna Loaf Make a cylinder shape. Point the ends and make one long slash lengthways down the centre.

Long Crusty Make a cylinder shape. Take a sharp pair of kitchen scissors and make diagonal cuts about 4cm/1½in long and downwards into the dough to a depth of about 2.5cm/1in to make a zig-zag pattern down the centre of the loaf. The cuts will spread apart as the loaf bakes.

Pain Brie Make a cylinder and taper it at each end. Make four parallel slashes down the length of the loaf.

Polka Make an elongated cylinder and score the surface to make a diagonal chequerboard pattern.

Baguette Roll the loaf into a long cylinder. Make four or five diagonal slashes down the loaf. Stagger them slightly.

BREAD ROLLS

You can divide the basic bread dough into small pieces to make all kinds of interestingly shaped rolls. As a general rule, bread dough made with 500g/1lb 2oz flour makes 16 rolls.

Round Rolls Divide the dough into small pieces. Place a piece of dough in the palm of one hand and roll the other hand, held flat, in a circular motion over the top. Round rolls can be left plain or can be slashed with one straight cut through the centre, a cross-cut or several short, parallel lines.

Rings Make a round roll. Push your finger through the centre and gently enlarge the hole to cover about one-third of the area.

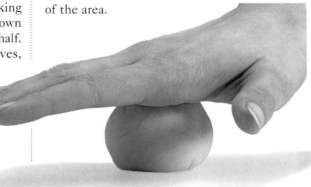

Long Rolls Form the dough into a ball and then roll the ball between your hands to make a cylinder. Gently taper the ends.

Clover Leaf On a bun tin, put three round rolls together in a clover leaf shape.

To make clover leaf rolls, three small balls of dough are placed close together on the bun tin so that they join together as they cook.

Circle On a baking sheet, arrange eight rolls in a circle touching each other, so that they stick together when baked.

Knots Make the dough into a long cylinder and tie it in a loose knot, taking care not to stretch it.

Parker House Rolls Roll all the dough to a thickness of about 12mm/½in. Cut it into 9cm/3½in rounds with a pastry cutter. Brush them with melted butter. Score down the centre of each circle with a sharp knife and fold the circle in half along the score. Put the rolls on a baking tray and gently press them down slightly.

BREAD FINISHES

Bread dough can be baked as it is, or it can be given attractive toppings and glazes. Most loaves are coated or glazed immediately after shaping.

Flour Coating Dust the loaf with extra flour after shaping for an attractive, 'country style' appearance.

Egg Glaze After shaping, brush the loaf with beaten egg.

Egg and Milk Glaze Beat together 1 egg and 2tbsp milk. This gives a less shiny surface than egg alone.

Milk and Sugar Glaze Use this for sweet buns. Warm 150ml/5fl oz milk and dissolve 1tbsp sugar in it.

BREAD TOPPINGS

A topping should be sprinkled onto a loaf after glazing but before slashing. It will add to the appearance of the loaf and also give a little added flavour to the crust. The most frequently used toppings are cracked wheat (usually on wholewheat bread), poppy seeds, sesame seeds, caraway seeds and cumin seeds. Flaked almonds and chopped nuts can be scattered over the top of sweet breads.

Different toppings – such as cracked wheat, chopped nuts, caraway seeds, sesame seeds, cumin seeds, flaked almonds and poppy seeds – can change the appearance of many breads and rolls, as well as adding flavour and texture.

35

CHAPTER ONE

PLAIN BREAD AND ROLLS

ave fun exploring different cultures by experimenting with simple, basic mixtures of flour, yeast and liquid to produce an astonishing variety of plain bread and rolls. Size and shape, and kneading, rising and baking methods, all have their effect on the texture, flavour and colour of the finished loaf.

PLAIN BREAD AND ROLLS

Plain bread has long been the staple food in most parts of the world. The peasant bread of Spain, baked in large loaves, has been unchanged for several centuries. In contrast, the Italian ciabatta bread, shaped like a slipper and with a ripe, yeasty flavour, is one of the newest breads to be devised. In between, there is the crispy baguette, now almost synonymous with France, and two American breads, Salt Risin' Bread, made from cornmeal and bicarbonate of soda, on lonely farmsteads, where yeast was unavailable, and Fannie Farmer's Water Bread, light and white but long-keeping and created in a cooking school in Boston. A plain bread dough can also be made into small rolls for individual portions. There are the light, soft rolls, made with small amounts of egg or milk, rolls for which the dough can be kept in the refrigerator until you need it, dense, delicious bagels — which are first boiled then baked — and traditional English muffins, cooked on a griddle.

Die Rast der Schnitter, *Pieter Brueghel (1564-1638)*

39

ENGLISH MUFFINS

English muffins are made with a moist yeast dough and baked on a griddle (a heavy iron plate). To serve them, make a slit in each side of the muffin without splitting them apart. Toast them on each side. After toasting, pull them in two and butter the soft, inner side. Muffins should be eaten on the day they are made.

MAKES 12 MUFFINS

200ml • 7fl oz warm water
30g • 1oz fresh yeast or 2tsp
  dried yeast
1tsp sugar
1kg • 2lbs 4oz strong, plain
  white flour or half white and
  half wholewheat flour

1tbsp salt
200ml • 7fl oz warm milk
30g • 1oz butter, softened
rice flour for dusting
butter or oil for greasing
  griddle

Put the water into a small bowl and sprinkle in the yeast and sugar. Leave fresh yeast for 5 minutes and dried for 15 minutes.

Put the flour into a bowl and mix in the salt. Make a well in the centre. Pour in the yeast and milk and add the butter. Beat the ingredients together thoroughly using a wooden spoon and then knead by hand in the bowl until the dough feels smooth and elastic. Cover the bowl with a clean cloth and leave it in a warm place for 1 hour, or until it has doubled in size.

Knead the dough again into a bowl and divide it into 12 portions. Coat a work surface with rice flour. Turn each portion separately in the flour to coat, then shape it into either a round or a square shape. Leave the muffins on the work surface, cover them with a clean cloth, and let them prove for 20 minutes.

Brush a cast-iron griddle with oil or melted butter. Warm the griddle on a low heat and place on it as many muffins as will fit without touching. (Use a fish slice to transfer them.) Cook the muffins slowly, for about 8-10 minutes on each side. They should be a biscuit colour and sound hollow when tapped. Re-grease the griddle lightly between each batch, if necessary.

When the muffins are done, wrap them in a thick cloth until they are cool.

Pot Bread

Pot bread was created in South Africa in the nineteenth century by the Dutch Voortrekkers travelling across the country in open wagons. They carried supplies of flour, but had no ovens. One of their essential pieces of equipment, however, was a heavy, cast-iron cooking pot with a lid and three legs. Sourdough leaven was used to make a dough, and when it was risen it was placed in the pot and covered with the lid. The problem of where to bake the loaf was solved by excavating a convenient anthill, heating the inside with a wood fire, and placing the covered pot in it. Later, the three-legged pot was replaced by one with a flat base and straight sides, which could be placed in the ashes of a camp fire.

Pot bread is still popular today. To make it, use an ordinary, plain bread dough, place it in an oiled, cast-iron casserole and cover with the lid. In South Africa, a casserole containing pot bread is often baked in a fire pit and served at a braai,

A BOER FARM.

or barbecue. It can also be put into an oven set at 200° C/400° F/gas mark 6 for 40 minutes.

The loaf will rise to the shape of the pot and the top will be slightly cracked. Baking in a closed container produces a very yeasty flavour.

REFRIGERATOR ROLLS

These rolls are raised by yeast and the action of the long fermenting process on the potatoes. The dough can be made up in the conventional way and used immediately, or it can be kept for at least a week in the refrigerator and can also be frozen for up to one month. Keeping a store of this dough is a good way to have freshly made rolls every day, without having to wait for the dough to rise. You can simply go to the refrigerator and take out the required amount of dough. Once cooked, the rolls have a very light texture and are best eaten when they are fresh.

MAKES 20–24 ROLLS

175g • 6oz potatoes (not new)	*1tsp salt*
165ml • 5¹/₂fl oz warm water	*125ml • 4fl oz warm milk*
30g • 1oz fresh yeast or	*1 egg, beaten*
15g • ¹/₂oz dried yeast	*60g • 2oz butter, cut into small*
560g • 1lb 4oz strong, plain	*pieces and softened*
white flour	OPTIONAL GLAZE
2tsp sugar	*1 egg beaten with 1tsp salt*

Clean the potatoes. Boil them in their skins until they are soft (this gives a better texture and flavour). Then peel and mash them and leave them to cool.

Put the water into a small bowl and sprinkle in the yeast. Leave fresh yeast for 5 minutes and dried for 15 minutes.

Put the flour into a large mixing bowl and toss in the sugar and salt. Make a well in the centre and pour in the yeast mixture, milk and egg. Add the butter. Mix to a dough. Leave for 5 minutes and then mix in the potatoes. Turn the dough onto a floured work surface. Knead it until it is smooth. Return the dough to the bowl.

You can now simply leave it to rise in a warm place, then shape and prove the rolls and bake them straight away, in which case cover the bowl with a clean cloth. Alternatively, you can put the bowl into the refrigerator and leave it for 12 hours or more, in which case cover it with plastic film.

After 12 hours in the refrigerator, the dough should have risen to the top of the bowl. If you are not going to use it immediately, punch it down, turn it over and make a cross-cut in the top for decoration. Cover the bowl again, return it to the refrigerator, and use the dough when needed. It will keep for up to one week.

To bake the refrigerated dough, knead it first on a floured work surface, return it to the bowl, cover it with a clean cloth and leave it in a warm place for 1–1½ hours, or until it has doubled in size. Heat the oven to 220°C/425°F/gas mark 7. Knead the dough again and form it into rolls (20–24 if using the whole amount at one time). Place them on floured baking sheets, brush them with the glaze, if using, and leave them in a warm place for 15 minutes to prove.

Bake the rolls for 15 minutes, or until they are golden brown. Transfer onto wire racks to cool.

FANNIE FARMER'S WATER BREAD

This is the first loaf in the 'Bread and Bread Making' section of *The Original Boston Cooking School Cookbook* by Fannie Merritt Farmer. Its characteristics are the use of boiling water to dissolve the butter, lard, sugar and salt, and the long rising time, which produces a rich flavour, and which may well have been necessary in 1896 when the standard of yeast was variable. Fannie Farmer uses lard so as not to spoil the whiteness of the bread with too much butter, but vegetarians can use all butter if wished. What Fannie Farmer calls 'biscuits' are more like small, flat rolls.

MAKES ONE 1KG · 2LBS 4OZ LOAF PLUS 15 BISCUITS

15g · ½oz butter	*30g · 1oz fresh yeast or*
15g · ½oz lard	*15g · ½oz dried yeast*
1tbsp sugar	*4tbsp warm water*
1½tsp salt	*750g · 1½lb strong, plain*
500ml · 18fl oz boiling water	*white flour*

Put the butter, lard, sugar and salt into a large bowl and pour on the boiling water. Stir to dissolve the ingredients and then leave until the liquid is lukewarm. Stir the yeast into the warm water and add 625g/1¼lb of the flour. Knead the mixture in the bowl until it is thoroughly mixed and then knead in the remaining flour.

Turn the dough onto a floured work surface and knead it until it is smooth. Return it to the bowl and cover it with a clean cloth. Leave it to rise overnight in a temperature of about 17°C/63°F.

In the morning, heat the oven to 200°C/400°F/gas mark 6. Make several slashes in the dough with a sharp knife and turn it over. Repeat the slashing and turning several times. Turn the dough onto a floured work surface and knead it again. Take off two-thirds of the dough, shape it and put it into a greased loaf tin. Roll the remaining dough to a thickness of 12mm/½in and stamp it into 5cm/2in rounds with a biscuit cutter. This quantity will make about 15. Place them on a floured board. Leave the loaf until it has risen above the top of the tin and the biscuits until they are slightly puffy.

Bake the loaf for 40 minutes and the biscuits for 15 minutes, or until both are golden brown and risen. Transfer them onto wire racks to cool.

PEASANT BREAD

This type of bread is typical of the everyday bread that is eaten throughout Spain. It is firm-textured and springy, with a crisp crust. Here it is made into a large tear shape that is characteristic of the bread of the northern regions. Around Andalusia, loaves are often oblong with slashed tops, and large, cushion-shaped loaves can be found all over the country. Frequently, peasant bread is stamped with the mark of the baker.

MAKES ONE 1KG · 2LBS 4OZ LOAF

750g · 1½lb strong, plain	*30g · 1oz fresh yeast or*
white flour	*15g · ½oz dried yeast*
500ml · 18fl oz warm water	*1tbsp salt*
2tbsp milk	

Put the flour into a bowl, reserving approximately 60g/2oz. Leave it in a warm place for about 15 minutes. Put 150ml/¼pt of the warm water into a small bowl with the milk. Sprinkle in the yeast and leave it in a warm place for 5 minutes if fresh and 15 minutes if dried.

Make a well in the flour and pour in the yeast mixture. Leave it without stirring and sprinkle the remaining flour over the top. Cover the dough with a cloth and leave in a warm place for 1 hour or until the yeast is frothy.

With your hand, knead the flour into the yeast from the edges of the well outwards, until a fairly dry dough has formed in the centre. Sprinkle the salt around the flour that is still dry and then gradually add the remaining water to the well, drawing in the flour from the edges as you work. When all the water has been added and the dough is evenly mixed, turn the dough onto a floured work surface and knead it until it is smooth and soft. Return the dough to the bowl. Cover it with a cloth and leave it in a warm place for 1 hour, or until it has doubled in size.

Heat the oven to 200°C/400°F/gas mark 6. Knead the dough again and form it into a long oval shape about 47cm/18in long and narrower at one end than the other. Place it on a floured baking sheet and flatten it slightly. Leave it in a warm place until it has doubled in size.

Bake the loaf for 45 minutes, or until the top is golden brown and it sounds hollow when tapped. Lift the loaf onto a wire rack to cool.

SOFT ROLLS

Bread rolls can be made with a basic bread dough. However, if small amounts of extra ingredients are added, such as milk, eggs or fat, the texture becomes much softer. The ingredients can be varied to suit availability and taste.

MAKES 16 ROLLS

165ml • 5½fl oz warm water
30g • 1oz fresh yeast or
   15g • ½oz dried yeast
560g • 1lb 4oz strong, plain
   white flour

2tsp salt
45g • 1½oz lard
180ml • 6fl oz warm milk

Put the water into a small bowl and sprinkle in the yeast. Leave fresh yeast for 5 minutes and dried for 15 minutes.

Put the flour and salt into a large mixing bowl and rub in the lard. Make a well in the centre and pour in the yeast and the milk. Mix to a dough. Turn the dough onto a floured work surface and knead it until it is smooth. Return the dough to the bowl. Cover it with a clean cloth and leave it in a warm place for 1 hour or until it has doubled in size.

Heat the oven to 200°C/400°F/gas mark 6. Knead the dough again and divide it into 16 pieces. Form each piece into a roll shape (for shapes see pages 32–5). Put the rolls onto floured baking sheets and leave them in a warm place for 15 minutes to prove.

Bake the rolls for 20 minutes, or until they are golden brown. Instead of cooling them on a rack, keep them soft by wrapping them in a thick cloth so that the steam is kept in as they cool.

Variations

Use a wholewheat bread flour, or a mixture of half white and half wholewheat, for a healthy alternative.

•

Use shortening or butter instead of lard and replace 60ml • 2fl oz of the liquid with 1 beaten egg and add it with the milk for an even softer result.

•

Instead of milk, use 200ml • 7fl oz water and 2 beaten eggs and add the eggs when you would add the milk to make a rich and luxurious version.

The Sandwich

The combination of bread and meat or bread and cheese, with the emphasis on the bread, has been a standard meal for many centuries, probably almost since bread was first made. Putting the meat or cheese between two pieces of bread made the meal easy to carry and easy to handle and must have been practised from an early time. French farm-workers in medieval times would eat a piece of meat between two pieces of coarse bread, and similar meals were common in Mediterranean lands.

This people's meal went upmarket in England in the eighteenth century, taking its name from John Montague, Earl of Sandwich. There are two reasons given why this came about, but the truth is not known for certain. One story is that the earl was an inveterate gambler who couldn't bear to leave the gaming table, even to eat. So to keep his master well fed, his cook put meat, and probably pickles, between two slices of buttered bread. The other tale says that Montague was a keen sportsman who preferred to carry his lunch with him when hunting or shooting.

Whichever is right, the new name gave what then became 'the sandwich' a new lease of life and sandwiches were often served at smart buffets laid on by the English gentry in the eighteenth century.

Since then, sandwiches have become common all over the world. The English put them in lunch-boxes, the French favour filling baguettes, the Scandinavians leave them open and the Americans stack them high.

FINNISH RYE BREAD *with* CARAWAY SEEDS

The combination of white flour and whole rye flour in this recipe produces a light-textured but well-flavoured loaf. It is a type of bread much liked in Finland; caraway seeds are a favourite flavouring throughout Scandinavia. The loaf is best eaten on the day it is made, and it goes well with either preserves or cheese.

MAKES ONE 750G · 1½LB LOAF

300ml • 10fl oz warm water
30g • 1oz fresh yeast or
  15g • ½oz dried yeast
1tbsp dark muscovado sugar
15g • ½oz butter, softened

250g • 9oz strong, plain
  white flour
180g • 6oz whole rye flour
1tbsp caraway seeds
1½tsp salt

Put half the water into a large mixing bowl and sprinkle in the yeast. Leave fresh yeast for 5 minutes and dried for 15 minutes. Stir in the remaining water, the sugar and butter. Mix the two types of flour together and add the caraway seeds and salt. Make a well in the centre and stir in the yeast liquid. Knead the mixture in the bowl until it begins to change texture. Cover the dough with a cloth and leave it in a warm place for 10 minutes. Turn it onto a floured work surface and knead it until it is smooth. Return the dough to the bowl. Cover and leave for 1 hour to double in size.

Heat the oven to 180°C/350°F/gas mark 4. Knead the dough again and form it into a round loaf by tucking the edges underneath. Place it on a floured baking sheet and leave it in a warm place for 20 minutes to prove.

Bake the loaf for 40 minutes, or until it has a hard, brown crust and sounds hollow when tapped. Lift it onto a wire rack to cool.

Bread-making Machines

With a bread-making machine you can have fresh bread to order – with a minimum of effort and just a little pre-planning.

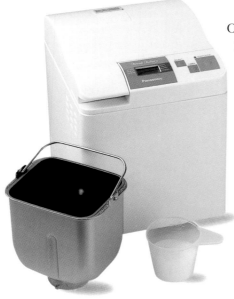

Once learned, the basic bread-making process is easy, but for the times when you do not have time to knead, shape and prove a loaf, there are machines available that will do all the work for you. With one of these you can make anything from a plain white loaf to croissants and Chelsea buns.

Bread-making machines are a fairly recent invention, but they are becoming more and more popular as people realise that, at a touch of a button, they can make bread when they choose. Kneading by hand is completely unnecessary, and as the

Bread-making machines usually come with all the necessary equipment for measuring and mixing.

process takes place in one container, there are no dishes to wash.

SETTINGS

Most machines have a choice of settings, enabling you to choose the type of bread you would like to bake and how much time you are going to spend on it.

The most basic setting allows you to put all the ingredients into the machine and then walk away until it is time to open the machine and take out the loaf. There is sometimes a faster version of this basic setting, which makes bread in even less time.

Some machines have a programme for adding ingredients. A beeper will sound when it is time to add dried fruits, or other such ingredients, so they are not crushed by the kneading process.

The 'dough' setting is used if you want the machine to mix and knead the dough for you, leaving you to take it out and shape it as you want. This is useful if you would rather make rolls instead of bread or if a loaf has to be baked in a characteristic tin such as a *Gugelhupf* mould.

Some machines have separate programmes for white and wholewheat or multigrain flours. They may also have programmes for adapting conventional recipes.

Tips for Using a Bread-making Machine

- *Always refer to the manufacturer's instructions before beginning a loaf. These will tell you the right programme to use.*
- *Keep the inside of the machine clean.*
- *Place the machine on a firm, dry worktop not covered with a tablecloth or any other textile. There should be a distance of at least 5cm/2in between the machine and the wall or any other object.*
- *Keep the machine out of reach of children.*
- *Do not use the machine near a heat source or in rooms where the humidity is high.*
- *Do not cover the machine when it is in use.*
- *Never remove the bread pan when the machine is in use. This upsets the programme.*
- *Use oven gloves when taking the bread out, as both machine and bread will be very hot.*

Timer

The basic bread-making programme is 3–5 hours. You can, however, set the timer for up to 13 hours. This is particularly useful if you are out all day and would like to come home to fresh bread, or if you would like to wake up to freshly baked bread for breakfast.

Ingredients

The same ingredients are used in a machine as for breads baked conventionally. You can choose the type of flour you use, provided you follow the methods and settings recommended by the manufacturer.

An easy-blend yeast is recommended. It is put directly into the bread pan and should never be mixed with cold water first. A fast-action, easy-bake yeast should be used with wholewheat flours.

Use ordinary table salt only, not a coarse sea salt or a low-sodium substitute.

If you are using fat, butter gives the best flavour and texture.

Liquids are used cold, not warm, as all the heating necessary is done by the machine. Milk can be used instead of water, but only dried milk can be used with the overnight programme.

Eggs and other fresh ingredients, such as chopped onion, can be added at the appropriate times (see manufacturer's instructions) but, like milk, should not be added to bread being baked on the timer setting because they might go stale during the long waiting period.

Basic White Loaf Recipe for a Bread-making Machine

Makes one 1kg • 2lb 4oz loaf

1tsp easy-bake yeast
500g • 1lb strong, plain white flour
1tbsp sugar
30g • 1oz butter
2tbsp dried milk powder
1½tsp table salt
360ml • 12fl oz cold water

Take the bread pan out of the machine and mount the kneading blade on the shaft.
Put the yeast in the bottom of the bread pan, then add the flour, sugar, butter, milk powder and salt.
Pour in the water.
Put the bread pan back into the machine, making sure it touches the bottom of the compartment.
Close the lid.
Plug in the machine.
Select the menu you want: for example, bake, rapid bake or timer.
Press start.
The machine will make a beep or other noise when the bread is ready. As soon as this happens, open the lid and take out the bread pan.
Turn the bread pan upside down and shake it several times to remove the loaf.
Place the loaf on a wire rack.
Unplug the machine and allow it to cool.

MIXED GRAIN BREAD

This type of bread, made with cracked wheat and a mixture of wholegrain flours, is a favourite in New Zealand, where rich, high-fibre breads are a popular part of a healthy diet. Cracked wheat is available from health food stores. The mix of ingredients and the single rising period produce a very loose-textured, moist, crumbly loaf that sometimes has holes running through it. This is a characteristic, and not a mistake in your baking! The flavour is on the sweet side because so little salt is added.

MAKES ONE 1KG · 2LBS 4OZ LOAF

125g · 4oz cracked wheat
600ml · 1pt cold water
500ml · 18fl oz warm water
30g · 1oz fresh yeast or
   15g · ½oz dried yeast

4tbsp skimmed milk powder
280g · 10oz wholewheat flour
280g · 10oz whole rye flour
1tsp salt

Put the cracked wheat into a saucepan and cover it with the cold water. Bring it to the boil, simmer it for 1 minute, remove it from the heat and drain it. Cool it to lukewarm.

Put about one-third of the warm water into a large mixing bowl and sprinkle in the yeast. Leave fresh yeast for 5 minutes and dried for 15 minutes. Stir in the remaining water, the skimmed milk powder and the cracked wheat. Mix the two types of flour together and add the salt. Gradually mix the flours into the wheat mixture to make a moist dough. Knead the dough in the bowl until it begins to change texture and become elastic.

Put the dough into a greased 1kg/2lbs 4oz loaf tin and leave it in a warm place for 30 minutes to 1 hour, or until it rises to about 12mm/½in above the edges of the tin. Meanwhile, heat the oven to 200°C/400°F/gas mark 6.

Bake the loaf for 45 minutes, or until it sounds hollow when tapped. Turn it onto a wire rack to cool.

MASSA SOVADA

Massa Sovada is another interestingly shaped, sweet bread. It comes from Portugal and the dough is rolled round in a spiral shape, known as a *caracois*, or 'snail'. The bread is firm-textured and sweet, and good with preserves or as an accompaniment to fruit compôtes. Day-old bread is also very good toasted.

MAKES ONE 750G · 1½LB LOAF

4tbsp warm water
15g · ½oz fresh yeast or
    2tsp dried yeast
375g · 13oz strong, plain
    white flour
90g · 3oz sugar
1tsp salt
90ml · 3fl oz warm milk
1 egg, beaten
45g · 1½oz unsalted butter, cut
    into small pieces and softened

Put the water into a small bowl and sprinkle in the yeast. Leave fresh yeast for 5 minutes and dried for 15 minutes.

Put two-thirds of the flour into a large mixing bowl and mix in the sugar and salt. Make a well in the centre. Pour in the yeast mixture, the milk and the beaten egg. Using your hand, gradually bring in flour from the sides of the well. Beat in the butter and then the remaining flour, a little at a time. Turn the dough onto a floured work surface and knead it until it is smooth. Return the dough to the bowl. Cover it with a clean cloth and leave it in a warm place for 1 hour, or until it has doubled in size.

Heat the oven to 180°C/350°F/gas mark 4. Knead the dough again and form it into a long length about 4cm/1½in in diameter. Flour a 23cm/9in diameter, shallow cake tin. Starting from the centre, spiral the length of dough inside it.

Leave the loaf in a warm place for 15 minutes to prove. Bake it for 40 minutes, or until it is golden brown and sounds hollow when tapped. Turn it onto a wire rack to cool.

SALT RISIN' BREAD

Salt Risin' Bread is an American farmhouse bread, made with bicarbonate of soda as a raising agent but left for a long time to rise and ferment like a yeast dough. Made with a mixture of cornmeal and plain cake flour, it has a dense texture, with a soft crumb and a thin, golden crust. It goes well with anything from sweet preserves to a rich stew. The long fermentation time precludes Salt Risin' Bread from being the kind of loaf that you would make daily, but it was originally made in the days when it was not unusual to make enough loaves in one batch to last one family for a week.

MAKES ONE 1KG · 2LBS 4OZ LOAF

60g · 2oz cornmeal
2tsp sugar
2tsp salt
250ml · 9fl oz milk, boiling
375g · 13oz plain, white
    cake flour
½tsp bicarbonate of soda
30g · 1oz lard or shortening

Put the cornmeal into a large mixing bowl with 1tsp each of the sugar and salt. Pour on the boiling milk. Cover the bowl and leave it in a warm place for 12 hours, by which time the batter should have started to form bubbles.

Mix in one-third of the flour, the remaining salt and sugar and the bicarbonate of soda. Cover the mixture again and leave it in a warm place to rise for 3 hours. It may well start to smell rather unpleasant at this stage, but this is just a product of the fermentation and will not give an unpleasant flavour to the loaf. By the end of the 3 hours, the mixture should have risen.

Heat the oven to 180°C/350°F/gas mark 4. In the bowl, knead in the remaining flour and the lard or shortening. Form the mixture into a loaf shape and put it into a greased 1kg/2lbs 4oz loaf tin. No further proving is needed.

Bake the loaf for 50 minutes, or until it is golden brown. Turn it onto a wire rack to cool.

49

PEINETA

Plain, sweetened breads called *pan dulce* have been popular in Mexico since the first sugar cane was grown there in the fifteenth century. The special attraction about *peineta*, translated as 'comb bread', is its interesting shape, similar to a cock's comb. It is soft, very slightly sweet and with a thin crust. It is best eaten with preserves.

MAKES ONE 750G · 1½LB LOAF

125ml · 4fl oz warm water	*30g · 1oz sugar*
15g · ½oz fresh yeast or 2tsp	*1 egg, beaten*
dried yeast	*440g · 15oz strong, plain*
90ml · 3fl oz warm milk	*white flour*
30g · 1oz lard, softened	*1tsp salt*

Put the water into a large mixing bowl and sprinkle in the yeast. Leave fresh yeast for 5 minutes and dried for 15 minutes. Add the milk, lard, sugar and egg. Mix the flour with the salt, stir it into the liquids and mix to a dough. Turn the dough onto a floured work surface and knead it until it is smooth. Return the dough to the bowl. Cover it with a clean cloth and leave it in a warm place for 1 hour, or until it has doubled in size.

Heat the oven to 180°C/350°F/gas mark 4. Knead the dough again and roll it into a round about 25cm/10in in diameter and 2cm/¾in thick. Lift the round onto a floured baking sheet. Using sharp kitchen scissors or a sharp knife, make slits all around the outside of the round, about 2cm/¾in long and 2cm/¾in apart. Fold the round nearly in half so that the upper layer is about 2.5cm/1in short of meeting exactly with the edge of the lower layer. Ease the corners backwards, away from the edges, so that the loaf becomes a crescent shape. Leave it in a warm place for 20 minutes to prove.

Bake the loaf for 30 minutes, or until the top is golden brown and sounds hollow when tapped. Lift the loaf onto a wire rack to cool.

Don Quixote

*With the bread eaten up, up breaks
the company.*

MIGUEL DE CERVANTES, 1547–1616

BAGUETTE

This is the classic long French loaf, crisp on the outside and soft in the middle, and always best eaten on the day that it is made. For the most authentic effect, baguettes should be made with a large proportion of ordinary cake flour rather than strong, white bread flour. In commercial bakeries, the crisp crust is achieved by jets of steam that are released inside the ovens. The steam causes the surface of the loaves to become initially very soft and then, when the steam is turned off, to become hard and crisp in the dry heat. A substitute for this method is to brush the loaves repeatedly with water as they bake.

MAKES 4 BAGUETTES, EACH APPROXIMATELY 35CM · 14IN LONG

450ml · 16fl oz warm water	*500g · 1lb 2oz plain, white*
30g · 1oz fresh yeast or	*cake flour*
15g · ½oz dried yeast	*90g · 3oz strong, plain*
1½tsp salt	*white flour*

Pour 150ml/5fl oz of the water into a small bowl and sprinkle in the yeast. Leave fresh yeast for 5 minutes and dried for 15 minutes. Dissolve the salt in the remaining water.

Mix the two types of flour together in a large mixing bowl. Make a well in the centre and pour in the yeast mixture. Mix in a little of the flour from the edges of the well. Gradually add the salted water, mixing in the flour as you do so.

Turn the dough onto a floured work surface (use cake flour rather than a strong type) and knead it until it is smooth. Return the dough to the bowl. Cover it with a clean cloth and leave it in a warm place for 1 hour, or until it has doubled in size.

Heat the oven to 200°C/400°F/gas mark 6 and place a baking tin of boiling water in the bottom of the oven. Knead the dough again and divide it into 4 pieces. Roll each piece into a long, thin loaf about 35cm/14in long and place it on a floured baking sheet. Leave the loaves in a warm place to prove for 30 minutes. Brush them with cold water and, with a sharp knife, make regular diagonal slashes along the length for a traditional appearance.

Bake the loaves for 1 hour, brushing them with cold water every 15 minutes. When done, they should be very crisp and golden. If they look like they are going to brown too quickly, cover them with crumpled aluminium foil.

Lift the loaves onto wire racks to cool. Eat them on the day of baking.

BAGELS

Bagels originated in Austria, where they were called *Beugeln*, meaning 'rings', referring to their shape. They have become a favourite food in Jewish communities all over the world, particularly in the United States and Australia. Bagels are dropped into boiling water before being baked and this gives them a firm, but light, texture and a shiny surface. Bagels are traditionally served split, spread with cream cheese and topped with smoked fish such as salmon or herring.

MAKES 16 BAGELS

250ml • 9fl oz warm milk
15g • ½oz fresh yeast or
   2tsp dried yeast
60g • 2oz butter, cut into small
   pieces and softened
30g • 1oz caster sugar
1 egg, separated

½tsp salt
440g • 15oz strong, plain
   white flour
oil for greasing
1tbsp poppy or sesame seeds or
   coarse salt for topping

Put the milk into a large mixing bowl and sprinkle in the yeast. Leave fresh yeast for 5 minutes and dried for 15 minutes.

Stir in the butter, sugar, egg white and salt. Then gradually mix in the flour to make a soft dough. Turn the dough onto a floured work surface and knead it until it is smooth. Return the dough to the bowl. Cover it and leave it in a warm place for 1 hour, or until it has doubled in size.

Heat the oven to 200°C/400°F/gas mark 6. Knead the dough again and divide it into 16 equal-sized pieces and form each piece into a round. To make the bagel shape, flour your forefinger and push it down through the centre of the round. Gently work it round in a circle to enlarge the hole. Make the hole bigger by twirling the bagel round and round, until it makes up about one-third of the diameter of the dough. When all the bagels are shaped, place them on a floured work surface, cover them with a cloth, and leave them to rise for 10 minutes. Cover three baking sheets with foil and lightly oil the foil. Bagels are wet and will stick if this is not done.

Bring a large pan of water to simmering point, so the water is just trembling. Maintain it at this temperature. Drop the bagels into the water, a few at a time so that they stay separate. Leave them in the water for about 15 seconds, or until they begin to swell. Lift them out with a perforated spoon and place them on the prepared baking sheets.

Brush the bagels with the egg yolk and scatter them with your chosen topping. Bake them for 20 minutes, or until they are golden brown. Transfer them to wire racks to cool. You may well find that, during cooking, the hole in the centre closes up and becomes simply an indentation.

OATMEAL *and* POTATO BREAD

This is based on a German recipe called *Kraftbrot mit Haferflocken. Kraftbrot* is usually bread made with white flour with added wheatgerm, and one of its uses is for open sandwiches. In this recipe, the wheatgerm has been replaced by rolled oats. The addition of potatoes makes the bread springy and close-textured, and the crust is thin and golden. It certainly makes very good open sandwiches.

MAKES ONE 1KG • 2LBS 4OZ LOAF

155g • 5oz potatoes (not new)
15g • ½oz butter
300ml • 10fl oz warm water
30g • 1oz fresh yeast or
   15g • ½oz dried yeast

500g • 1lb 2oz strong, plain
   white flour
155g • 5oz rolled oats

Wash the potatoes. Boil them in their skins until they are tender (this will give a better flavour and texture). Drain and peel them and mash them with the butter.

Put the water into a large mixing bowl and sprinkle in the yeast. Stir in the flour to make a moist dough. Cover the dough with a cloth and leave it in a warm place for 1 hour to double in size.

Heat the oven to 180°C/350°F/gas mark 4. Add the rolled oats and potatoes to the dough. Turn the dough onto a floured work surface and knead it for about 15 minutes, or until it is smooth and bubbles appear in the surface. Shape the dough and put it into a greased 1kg/2lbs 4oz loaf tin. Leave it in a warm place for 30 minutes to prove.

Bake the loaf for 50 minutes, or until the top is golden brown and sounds hollow when tapped. Turn the loaf onto a wire rack to cool.

CIABATTA

Ciabatta is a relatively new bread that comes from around Lake Como in Italy. Ciabatta means 'slipper' and the bread is so called because of the shape of the loaves. The characteristic, nutty, slightly sour flavour is produced by the two long rising times. It rises well in the oven to make a beige-coloured loaf with a thin, soft crust, a soft, holey crumb and a springy texture.

MAKES TWO 750G · 1½LB LOAVES

600ml • 1pt warm water	*800g • 1lb 12oz strong, plain*
30g • 1oz fresh yeast or	*white flour*
15g • ½oz dried yeast	*1tbsp salt*
1tsp sugar (for dried yeast only)	*90ml • 3fl oz olive oil*

Put 150ml/5fl oz of the water into a small bowl and sprinkle in the yeast. Add the sugar if using dried yeast. Leave fresh yeast for 5 minutes or dried for 15 minutes.

Put about two-thirds of the flour into a large mixing bowl. Gradually stir in the yeast mixture, the olive oil and finally all the remaining water. Knead the mixture with your hand in the bowl, taking the sides of the mixture to the middle with one hand and turning the bowl with the other. It will be very moist, like a thick batter. Cover the dough with a clean cloth and leave it in a warm place for 4 hours. It should be bubbly and will have doubled in size.

Add the salt to the rest of the flour. With your hand, knead the salted flour into the dough still in the bowl. It will be a very wet mixture. Cover the bowl with a cloth again and leave it in a warm place for a further 1 hour.

Heat the oven to 220°C/425°F/gas mark 7. Coat two baking trays liberally with flour. Knead the dough in the bowl again and divide it into two with your hand. The dough will be moist but springy. Tip each piece out onto a prepared tray. If necessary, gently push the dough around the edges to make it slightly wider at one end than the other. Scatter it with more flour. Leave the loaves in a warm place for 10 minutes to prove.

Bake the loaves for 30 minutes, or until they are golden brown and risen, and sound hollow when tapped. Lift them onto wire racks to cool.

CHAPTER TWO

ENRICHED BREADS

The addition of savoury or sweet fillings – or of milk, eggs, butter, oil or sugar – gives a whole new dimenision to your skills. From the traditional to the newly created, enriched breads can be meals in themselves, substantial snacks or wickedly indulgent tea-time or coffee-time treats.

ENRICHED BREADS

Roll a sumptuous olive oil bread dough around a savoury or sweet filling and you have a loaf, originally from the Middle East, that is good to look at and tasty and substantial to eat. Roll out a similar dough and fold it round lard, spices, sugar and dried fruits and you have Lardy Cake, a rich, sweet treat from an English cottage. Bread dough can also make small, savoury parcels that can be baked or steamed. When the added ingredients are kneaded into the dough, the whole texture of the loaf changes. The Sally Lunn is rich and golden and almost cake-like in its lightness, the brioche is firmer textured and makes wonderful toast, and a freshly made croissant is light and flaky. Other breads – such as anchovy bread and Christmas fruit loaf – are both enriched and flavoured, with extra ingredients being kneaded into the dough. And from Switzerland comes a cheese and onion tart on a rich bread base.

Afternoon Tea, *Kate Greenaway 1886*

57

BRIOCHE

The brioche is the favourite rich bread of France. It is best eaten fresh and slightly warm but, when a day old, it makes excellent toast. The classic brioche is made in a conical, fluted tin with a small portion of dough on top of the main loaf. Large and small tins are available. However, if you do not have the right tins you can use ordinary round cake tins, small ring moulds or 750ml/1¼pt pudding basins for the larger brioches, and dariole moulds or individual soufflé dishes for the smaller ones.

MAKES 2 LARGE · 12 SMALL BRIOCHES

4tbsp warm water	*3 eggs, beaten*
15g · ½oz fresh yeast or 2 tsp	*185g · 6oz butter, cut into small*
dried yeast	*pieces and softened*
375g · 13oz strong, plain	GLAZE
white flour	*1 egg yolk beaten with*
1tsp salt	*1tsp water*

Put the water into a small bowl and sprinkle in the yeast. Leave fresh yeast for 5 minutes and dried for 15 minutes.

Put the flour into a bowl and add the salt. Make a well in the centre. Pour in the yeast mixture and stir a little of the flour into it. Stir in the beaten eggs and add the butter. Mix to a dough.

Turn the dough onto a floured work surface and knead it until it is smooth and all the butter has become incorporated. Return the dough to the bowl. Cover it with a clean cloth and leave it in a warm place for 1 hour, or until it has doubled in size.

Knead the dough again. Return it to the bowl, cover it and chill it for at least 1 hour. This firms the butter and makes shaping the dough easier.

Heat the oven to 200°C/400°F/gas mark 6. Grease 2 large or 12 small brioche tins. Knead the dough lightly once more. Divide the dough into the right number of portions to suit your tins. For a classic brioche shape, divide the dough for each brioche into pieces of two-thirds and one-third of the bulk. Form the larger piece into a round and put it into the prepared tin. Make a hole in the centre. Shape the smaller piece into a cylinder, wider at the top than the bottom. Insert the narrow end into the hole in the larger piece of dough so that the end protrudes and looks like a round of dough sitting on the top.

Leave the brioches in a warm place for 30 minutes, or until the base has risen to the top of the tin. Brush the tops with the egg-and-water glaze. Bake large brioches for 25 minutes and small ones for 10 minutes. Turn them onto wire racks to cool.

The King's Breakfast

The King asked
The Queen, and
the Queen asked
the Dairymaid:
'Could we have some butter for
The Royal slice of bread?'

A. A. MILNE, 1882–1956

ROLLED BREAD

Roll a delicious and easy bread dough, enriched with olive oil, round a choice of simple fillings and you can create an attractive and tasty loaf. Those made with savoury fillings are a tempting, easy snack or an exciting accompaniment to cheese, salads, casseroles or soups. Rolled bread with a sweet filling can be served with coffee or tea, mid-morning or mid-afternoon.

MAKES TWO 40CM · 16IN LONG LOAVES

300ml • 10fl oz warm water
15g • ½oz fresh yeast or
  2tsp dried yeast
2tbsp olive oil

500g • 1lb 2oz strong, plain
  white flour
½tsp salt

Put the water into a large mixing bowl and sprinkle in the yeast. Leave fresh yeast for 5 minutes and dried for 15 minutes. Add the oil. Stir in the flour and salt. Form the mixture into a dough. Turn it onto a floured work surface and knead it well. Return it to the bowl and cover it with a clean cloth. Leave it in a warm place for 1 hour, or until it has doubled in size.

Prepare your chosen filling (see below). Heat the oven to 190°C/375°F/gas mark 5.

Knead the dough again and divide it into two equal pieces. Roll each piece into a rectangle about 20 × 40cm/ 8 × 16in. Spread the filling evenly over each piece of dough. Roll up the pieces of dough from one long side. Place the rolled loaves, join downwards, on a floured baking sheet. Pinch the ends to seal them and make a pointed shape. With a sharp knife, cut several slashes on each loaf.

Leave the loaves in a warm place for 20 minutes to prove. Bake them for 30 minutes, or until they are golden brown and sound hollow when tapped. Lift them onto wire racks to cool.

Fillings

(each is enough for 2 loaves)

Cheese and Onion Filling

2 medium onions, finely chopped
3tbsp olive oil
125g • 4oz feta cheese

Soften the onions in the olive oil over a medium heat. Spread them evenly over the dough. Cut the cheese into very small, thin slivers and scatter them over the top.

Herb and Garlic Filling

6tbsp fresh chervil or parsley, chopped
2tbsp fresh tarragon, chopped
2tbsp fresh thyme, chopped
2 garlic cloves, chopped
4tbsp olive oil

Mix all the ingredients together and spread them evenly over the two pieces of dough.

Olive Filling

2 medium onions, finely chopped
3tbsp olive oil
20 black olives

Soften the onions in the oil over a medium heat and divide them between the two pieces of dough. Stone and halve the olives and scatter them evenly over the top.

Walnut and Date Filling

90g • 3oz walnuts, shelled
125g • 4oz dates, stoned
1tsp ground cinnamon
60g • 2oz butter, melted

Very finely chop or grind the walnuts. Finely chop the dates. Put them into a bowl and mix in the cinnamon and melted butter. Spread the filling evenly over the dough.

CROISSANTS

The croissant was devised in Austria but has come to be associated far more with France. The yeast dough for croissants is easy to make, but combining it with butter, which has to be chilled to produce the flaky, layered texture, makes the process quite time-consuming. In France, croissant bakers put their dough into special cabinets that change temperature at regular intervals. To make croissants at home, the dough must be taken in and out of the refrigerator. The end result, however, is worth it, when golden croissants come out of the oven, crispy and flaky on the outside and soft in the middle.

MAKES ABOUT 15 CROISSANTS

250ml • 9fl oz warm water	*2tbsp sugar*
30g • 1oz fresh yeast or 1tbsp dried yeast	*1tsp salt*
625g • 1lb 5oz strong, plain white flour	*275g • 10oz butter, chilled*
	180ml • 6fl oz warm milk
	1 egg, beaten

Put the water into a small bowl and sprinkle in the yeast. Leave fresh yeast for 5 minutes and dried for 15 minutes.

Put the flour into a large mixing bowl and toss in the sugar and salt. Rub in 60g/2oz of the butter. Make a well in the centre and pour in the yeast mixture and the milk. Mix to a dough. Turn it onto a floured work surface and knead it until it is smooth. Return the dough to the bowl and cover it with plastic film. Put the dough into the refrigerator for 1 hour.

Put the remaining butter into a large polythene bag or between two pieces of plastic film and pound it with a rolling pin until it makes a flat rectangle about 23 × 2.5cm/9 × 5in. Knead the dough and roll it into a rectangle of about 46 × 25cm/18 × 10in. Place the rectangle of butter in the centre of the dough. Fold over the ends of the dough and then the sides. Roll the resulting packet lengthways into a rectangle and then fold it into three. Either put the folded dough into a polythene bag or wrap in plastic film. Put it into the refrigerator for 10 minutes. Roll and chill three times more. Heat the oven to 200°C/400°F/gas mark 6.

After the final chilling, roll the dough into a square about 5mm/¼in thick and then cut it into twelve 15cm/6in equilateral triangles. With a rolling pin, roll each triangle from base to tip to elongate it slightly. Then gently pull out the corners of the base so they stick out. Roll up the triangle from the base to the tip. Place the rolled dough on a floured baking sheet so the tip is underneath, then bring the ends round to make a crescent shape.

Leave the croissants uncovered to prove for 30 minutes. Just before baking, glaze them with the beaten egg. Bake the croissants for 15 minutes, or until they are golden brown. They should have risen in the oven and the tip will have pulled itself out to lie across the top. Cool the croissants on wire racks and serve them just warm.

Variations

For added variety, croissants can be filled with small amounts of sweet or savoury ingredients.
Place the fillings on the bottom half of the croissant before rolling. Only small amounts are needed.

Chocolate Croissants

You need thin pieces of chocolate only, so break off two squares of chocolate from a block (dark chocolate is best) and cut them in half lengthways. Place the strips of chocolate lengthways across the base of the triangle of dough before rolling up.

Almond Croissants

Mix 4tbsp ground almonds with 1tbsp honey and a few drops of almond essence. Put 2tsp on the base of each triangle.

Apple Croissants

Put 1tbsp puréed apple on the base of each triangle.

Cheese Croissants

Put 1tbsp grated Gruyère cheese on the base of each triangle.

Cheese and Ham Croissants

Put 1tbsp grated cheese and 1tbsp finely chopped lean ham on the base of each triangle.

Gugelhupf

For over 500 years, the Viennese have had a reputation for making fine bread, yeasted cakes and pastries. They like to gather in coffee houses morning or afternoon to enjoy a wide variety of sweet treats.

One of the most traditional yeasted cakes is the Viennese Gugelhupf. Cookery books have a number of spellings, including 'kugelhopf' and 'gugelkopf', but they all mean the same thing: a rich, sweet, yeasted cake, baked in a fluted, decorated mould.

A Gugelhupf can be plain or can contain ingredients such as nuts, dried fruit or candied peel. The dough can be flavoured with almond, lemon or vanilla, or part of it may be mixed with chocolate to produce a marbled effect. A Gugelhupf is usually sprinkled liberally with icing sugar when cool.

Emperor Franz Joseph I of Austria fell in love with Frau Katherina Schratt, an actress at the Burg Theatre. He visited her every day at 4.30 in the afternoon, the time when she would be taking from the oven the small, individual Gugelhupf of which he was so fond.

The Gugelhupf has another claim to fame. Marie Antoinette's mother was Austrian and the young queen had a particular liking for the cake of her ancestral country. When, just before the French Revolution, she suggested that the starving peasants eat cake instead of bread, she was referring to Gugelhupf.

SALLY LUNN

The Sally Lunn is a rich bread, usually round, which is served split crossways and thickly buttered. The name is probably a corruption of the French *soleil et lune* ('sun and moon') sometimes shortened to *solileme*, the name for a similar bread in France. In England, the name became Sally Lunn, and a legend grew up about a lady of the same name who sold home-made cakes from a shop in Bath in the eighteenth century. Sally Lunn bread has a very light, almost cake-like texture, a thin crisp crust and a golden crumb. Made without flavourings, it can be served either with preserves or with cheese. The lemon rind and candied peel are nineteenth-century additions and give the loaf more of a tea-cake flavour. Although rich, a Sally Lunn is quick to make as there is only one rising time.

MAKES ONE 500G · 1LB 2OZ LOAF

4tbsp warm water	*grated rind ½ lemon (optional)*
1tsp sugar	*2tbsp chopped candied peel*
15g · ½oz fresh yeast or	*(optional)*
2tsp dried yeast	*2 eggs, beaten*
butter for greasing	*125ml · 4fl oz double cream*
250g · 9oz strong, plain	*4tbsp milk*
white flour	GLAZE
½tsp salt	*1tbsp each milk and sugar*

Put the water into a small bowl and stir in the sugar. Sprinkle in the yeast. Leave fresh yeast for 5 minutes and dried for 15 minutes. Butter a 18cm/7in diameter, high-sided cake tin. Heat the oven to 200°C/400°F/gas mark 6.

Put the flour into a large mixing bowl. Add the salt and the lemon rind and/or the candied peel if you are using it. Make a well in the centre and pour in the yeast mixture, eggs, cream and milk. Knead the mixture with your hand to make a very moist dough.

Transfer the dough to the prepared tin and leave in a warm place for about 30 minutes, or until it has doubled in size. Bake the loaf for 30 minutes, or until it is risen and golden brown. For the glaze, dissolve the sugar in the milk. Brush it over the top of the cooked loaf and put the loaf back into the oven for 1 minute for the glaze to dry. Cool the loaf in the tin for 5 minutes and then put it onto a wire rack for a further 10 minutes.

To serve, cut the loaf into three pieces crossways, spread each piece thickly with butter, and then sandwich the pieces back together again. Cut the loaf into thin slices downwards; serve it with preserves or cheese or as an accompaniment to fruit compôtes.

SALAMI, CHEESE *and* ONION TART

This rich tart using a bread base is similar to ones made in Switzerland. The filling should sink into the base, making the centre moist and full of flavour and keeping the edges crisp. Serve the tart warm as a light meal or cold for snacks and picnics.

MAKES ONE 25CM · 10IN TART

180ml · 6fl oz warm water
15g · ½oz fresh yeast or
　2tsp dried yeast
275g · 10oz strong, plain
　white flour
1tsp salt
60g · 2oz butter, cut into small
　pieces and softened

FILLING
2 medium onions
30g · 1oz butter
60g · 2oz Italian salami
250g · 9oz Gruyère cheese
2 eggs
150ml · 5fl oz single cream
4tbsp milk

Put the water into a large mixing bowl and sprinkle in the yeast. Leave fresh yeast for 5 minutes and dried for 15 minutes. Mix together the flour and salt. Add them to the yeast mixture. Begin to mix them in and then add the butter. Mix to a dough. Turn the dough onto a floured work surface and knead it until it is smooth. Return the dough to the bowl. Cover it with a clean cloth and leave it in a warm place for 1 hour, or until it has doubled in size.

For the filling, thinly slice the onions and soften them in the butter on a low heat. Cut the salami into small pieces. Grate the cheese. Beat the eggs with the cream and milk.

Heat the oven to 200°C/400°F/gas mark 6. Knead the dough again and roll it into a round which is big enough to line a 25cm/10in tart tin. Place the dough in the tin and then cover it with half the cheese, half the salami, all the onions then the remaining cheese and salami. Pour in the egg and cream mixture.

Leave the tart for 20 minutes in a warm place. Bake it for 20 minutes, or until the top of the filling is golden. Take the tart from the tin as soon as it is cooked. Serve it warm or leave it to cool completely.

Sorrows of Werther

Werther had a love for Charlotte
Such as words could never utter;
Would you know how first he met her?
She was cutting bread and butter.

WILLIAM MAKEPEACE THACKERAY,
1811–1863

SUN-DRIED TOMATO BREAD

Since the recent popularity of sun-dried tomatoes, different types of tomato bread have been appearing in shops and supermarkets. There is no classic recipe for this, but most are made with white flour and enriched with olive oil.

MAKES ONE 750G · 1½LB LOAF

180ml · 6fl oz warm water	*1tsp salt*
15g · ½oz fresh yeast or 2tsp dried yeast	*1tbsp fresh oregano, chopped or 1tsp dried oregano*
125g · 4oz sun-dried tomatoes in oil	*1tbsp fresh thyme, chopped or 1tsp dried thyme*
375g · 13oz strong, plain white flour	*1 egg, beaten*
	90ml · 3fl oz olive oil

Put the water into a small bowl and sprinkle in the yeast. Leave fresh yeast for 5 minutes and dried for 15 minutes. Drain and finely chop the tomatoes.

Put the flour into a bowl. Mix in the salt and herbs. Make a well in the centre. Pour in the yeast mixture and the egg. Mix to a dough. Turn the dough onto a floured work surface and knead it until it is smooth. Gradually knead in the olive oil, about 1tbsp at a time. Divide the dough into two pieces. Knead the tomatoes into one piece only. Put the pieces of dough into separate bowls. Cover them with a clean cloth and leave them in a warm place for 1 hour, or until they have doubled in size.

Heat the oven to 200°C/400°F/gas mark 6. Oil a 20cm/8in diameter cake tin. Knead each piece of dough separately and divide it into 8 small pieces, to make 16 in all. Arrange the pieces in a chequerboard pattern in the cake tin. Leave the tin in a warm place for 20 minutes for the bread to prove.

Bake the loaf for 25 minutes, or until it is firm and sounds hollow when tapped but has not browned. Turn it out onto a wire rack to cool. To eat, pull off pieces of herb-flavoured and tomato bread separately.

65

Danish Pastries

Danish pastries are made in many parts of the world and go by a variety of names. All have light, flaky pastry, while the shapes and fillings vary.

Folding and rolling the chilled dough is an essential step in the making of light and flaky Danish pastries.

Copenhagen in Denmark is thought by some to be the city where Danish pastries were first made.

Danish pastries are made with light, flaky pastry, elaborately shaped, filled with just enough sweet filling and topped with a little icing. While English-speaking countries call them Danish pastries, the Danish call them *Wienebrot* (Vienna bread) and the Germans *Kopenhagener* (from Copenhagen). Like many such delicacies, their origins are disputed.

One story is that, in the nineteenth century, the bakers of Copenhagen went on strike and demanded cash wages instead of their customary room and board. They were all fired and were replaced by bakers from Germany and Austria, whose expertise was in making sweet, yeasted cakes.

The other, usually more accepted, explanation goes back to the sixteenth century, when a young French baker by the name of Claudius Gelée was making brioches and forgot to add the butter. When his master came in, he quickly folded the dough over the tell-tale butter that was lying on the worktop. He then kept rolling and folding until all the butter had been incorporated into the dough. When he cooked the dough, the surprise result was flaky pastry. Using his serendipitous discovery, Claudius Gelée opened his own bakery in Paris. He was later invited to Florence by two Italian bakers, brothers by the name of Mosca.

The Mosca brothers took the recipe several stages forward by developing different shapes and fillings, and it was not long before the pastries were also being made over the border in Austria.

Enter two young Danish bakers (their names have never been discovered) who travelled to Vienna to learn the secrets of good baking and who eventually took their new-found

Basic Recipe for Danish Pastries

Makes about 30 pastries

300ml • 10fl oz milk
200g • 7oz butter, chilled
30g • 1oz sugar
1 egg
1 egg yolk
45g • 1½ oz fresh yeast
500g • 1 lb 2oz strong, plain white flour
½ tsp salt
¼ tsp ground cardamom

Put the milk, 30g/1oz of the butter and all the sugar into a saucepan and heat gently. Stir until the butter has melted and the sugar dissolved. Cool to lukewarm. Beat in the egg and egg yolk, and crumble in the yeast. Put the flour into a bowl and toss in the salt and cardamom. Make a well in the centre and pour in the yeast mixture. Mix to a dough.
Turn the dough onto a floured work surface and knead it until it is smooth. Form the dough into a cube shape, put it into a polythene bag and chill it in the refrigerator for 30 minutes.
Put the remaining butter between two pieces of plastic film and hit it with a rolling in into a 20 x 10cm/8 x 4in rectangle. Take out the dough and roll into a rectangle measuring 40 x 20cm/16 x 8in. Place the butter in the centre and fold the sides of the dough over it. Roll out the dough to a rectangle 2cm/¾in thick. Fold the dough into three, replace it in the polythene bag and put it into the refrigerator for 10 minutes. Repeat this rolling, folding and chilling three more times.
After the final chilling, roll out the dough and fold it as before. Then cut it crossways into three pieces. It is now ready to be made into pastries of various shapes and with a choice of fillings.
To bake, lay the pastries on floured baking sheets and leave them in a warm place for 20 minutes to prove. Heat the oven to 200°C/400°F/gas mark 6. Bake the pastries for 20 minutes, or until they are golden brown. Cool them on wire racks.

knowledge home with them to Denmark. In Denmark, the pastries are mostly eaten at coffee-time.

Today, Danish pastries are made in many parts of the world, but there are still two specialities, produced with the same dough, that are made only in Denmark. One is Butter Cake, made in a round cake tin and consisting of a circle of dough topped with more dough made into circles, spirals or other elaborate shapes, the centre of which is then filled with a mixture of butter, sugar and sultanas. The other is the *Julekage* or 'Yule Cake', decorated with a star and filled with spiced, sweet custard, raisins and candied peel. Millions of *Julekage* are sold in the weeks running up to Christmas.

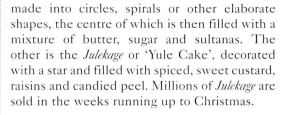

Danish Pastry Fillings

Each is enough for one-third of the dough (see recipe on left).

Spiced Sultana Filling

30g • 1oz caster sugar
1tsp ground cinnamon
30g • 1oz butter, softened
30g • 1oz sultanas

Beat the sugar and cinnamon into the butter and fold in the sultanas.

Almond Filling

60g • 2oz ground almonds
60g • 2oz caster sugar
1tbsp beaten egg
3 drops almond essence

Mix together the ground almonds and sugar in a bowl. Bind them together with the egg and beat in the almond essence.

Custard Cream Filling

1 egg yolk
1tbsp flour
1tsp cornflour
1tbsp sugar
150ml • 5fl oz milk
3 drops vanilla essence

Beat the egg yolk lightly in a bowl and work in the flour, cornflour, sugar and 4tbsp of the milk. Put the remaining milk into a saucepan and bring it to just below boiling point. Gradually stir the hot milk into the yolk mixture. Return the mixture to the saucepan and stir on a low heat to make a thick custard. Remove the custard from the heat and beat in the vanilla essence. Cool the mixture completely before using.

Decoration

The pastries can be served plain or drizzled with a simple icing made from 60g/2oz icing sugar and a little water. Halved glacé cherries, chopped nuts or flaked almonds may be sprinkled on top.

Some Danish Pastry Shapes

Here are some suggestions for shaping your pastries.

Snails

Roll out the dough to a 6mm/¼in thick rectangle and spread it evenly with the filling. Roll up the dough along one long side and cut it into 2.5cm/1in thick slices. Place the slices on a floured baking sheet.

Cock's combs

Roll the dough into a 20cm/8in rectangle. Spread half the width with the filling. Fold over the other half and cut the folded dough into 10cm/4in squares. Make three cuts in the folded side of the dough, from the fold to within 12mm/½in of the opposite side. Place the pastries on a floured baking sheet and gently spread out the sections.

Pinwheels

Roll out the dough to a thickness of 6mm/¼in and cut it into 15cm/6in squares. Cut from each corner to within 12mm/½in of the centre. Put a portion of the filling in the centre. Fold alternate sections to the middle so the points slightly overlap and seal them by gently pressing down in the centre.
Crescents, envelopes and twists are described in the section on bread shapes on page 32.

BLACKBERRY BREAD

In English cottages, blackberry bread was made in autumn, the wild blackberries making a cost-free substitute for expensive currants or raisins. Wholewheat flour was produced with the wheat gained from gleaning in the harvest fields. The bread is semi-sweet, moist and spicy, and streaked with purple from the blackberries. It is excellent, buttered, in a lunch box or as an afternoon snack.

MAKES ONE 1KG · 2LBS 4OZ LOAF

180ml · 6fl oz warm water
30g · 1oz fresh yeast or
   15g · ½oz dried yeast
500g · 1lb 2oz wholewheat
   flour
½tsp salt
½tsp ground cinnamon
¼ tsp nutmeg, freshly grated

1 egg, beaten
150ml · 5fl oz warm milk
2tbsp honey
45g · 1½oz lard or butter, cut
   into small pieces and softened
250g · 9oz blackberries, fresh,
   or frozen and just thawed

Put the water into a small bowl and sprinkle in the yeast. Leave fresh yeast for 5 minutes and dried for 15 minutes.

Put the flour into a large mixing bowl and mix in the salt, cinnamon and nutmeg. Make a well in the centre and put in the yeast, egg, milk, honey and lard. Mix to a moist dough. Add the blackberries and carefully mix them in. Knead the dough in the bowl, taking care not to squash the blackberries too much. Cover the dough with a clean cloth and leave it in a warm place for 1 hour, or until it has doubled in size.

Heat the oven to 200°C/400°F/gas mark 6. Turn the dough onto a floured work surface and knead it again. Form it into a loaf shape and put it into a 1kg/2lbs 4oz loaf tin.

Bake the loaf for 40 minutes, or until it sounds hollow when tapped and the top is just browned. Turn it onto a wire rack to cool.

CHRISTMAS FRUIT BREAD

This is a wholewheat version of the German Christmas speciality called the *Dresdner stollen*. It is fruity and spicy and good to serve for tea on Christmas Day.

MAKES ONE 1KG · 2LBS 4OZ LOAF

125ml · 4fl oz warm water
30g · 1oz fresh yeast or
   15g · ½oz dried yeast
500g · 1lb 2oz wholemeal flour
1tsp salt
60g · 2oz dark muscovado
   sugar
1tsp ground mixed spice
180ml · 6fl oz warm milk

1 egg, beaten
90g · 3oz butter, cut into small
   pieces and softened
90g · 3oz raisins
90g · 3oz sultanas
60g · 2oz chopped candied peel
60g · 2oz flaked almonds
2tbsp icing sugar, sieved

Put the water into a small bowl and sprinkle in the yeast. Leave fresh yeast for 5 minutes and dried for 15 minutes.

Put the flour into a bowl and mix in the salt, sugar and mixed spice. Make a well in the centre and pour in the yeast mixture and the milk. Add the egg and butter and mix to a dough. Turn it out onto a floured work surface and knead it until it is smooth. Gently knead in the dried fruit, candied peel and almonds.

Return the dough to the bowl. Cover it with a clean cloth and leave it in a warm place for 1 hour to double in size.

Heat the oven to 200°C/400°F/gas mark 6. Knead the dough again. Roll it into a rectangle about 30 × 20cm/12 × 8in. Fold the dough into three along the long sides. Place it on a floured baking sheet, join side down. With your hands, taper the ends of the loaf into points.

Leave the loaf in a warm place for 1 hour, or until it has doubled in size. Bake the loaf for 40 minutes, or until it sounds hollow when tapped and is a good brown colour. Lift it onto a wire rack to cool. When it has just cooled, coat it with the icing sugar.

68

Panettoni

The panettoni *is a loaf that originated in Lombardy, one of the richest regions in Italy, where butter rather than olive oil is the main cooking agent. It is a rich, yeasted cake, with a dome-shaped top said to resemble the cupolas of Lombardy churches. It is light in texture, yellow-coloured and contains sultanas and candied peel.*

The panettoni *is the food most often associated with Milan, the principal city of Lombardy. It is sold in most of the food shops and even at the windows of trains that stop in the main station. It was originally a Christmas treat but is now available at all times of the year. It can be eaten at any time of the day, although it is particularly popular with coffee at breakfast-time.*

The legend of the origin of panettoni *explains its name, which was once 'pan de Tonio', meaning 'Tony's bread'. Tonio was a baker who lived in the quarter of Milan known as Borogo delle Grazie in the fifteenth century and had a beautiful daughter called Adalgisa.*

A rich and well-connected young man, Ughetto della Tela, came courting Adalgisa, but Ughetto's family would not

accept her because her father was a tradesman. However, Ughetto discerned that it was not breeding that his father was looking for, but money, so he hatched a plan. Just before Christmas, Ughetto sold his hunting falcons to buy the baker flour, eggs and butter to make the traditional cakes of the region. He also added his own special touch, sultanas and candied lemon peel.

Tonio set about making his cakes. They were so good that everyone came to buy them and soon he was rich enough for Ughetto's family to accept Adalgisa.

69

Sheep's Cheese *and* Onion Bread

This is a variation of a German recipe, the original of which gave double the quantities here. The original recipe would have used a local sheep's milk cheese, but feta makes a good substitute. The amounts given below make a large, well-risen, oval loaf that is a meal in itself. The addition of the chopped raw onion might appear strange, but it steams gently in the heat of the baking dough and softens. The pieces of cheese melt, leaving the bread with a holey texture, a soft crumb and a delicious cheese flavour. Butter is optional and a crisp salad or a vegetable soup is all you need to make a satisfying meal.

MAKES ONE 1KG · 2LBS 4OZ LOAF

360ml · 12fl oz warm water
30g · 1oz fresh yeast or
   15g · ½oz dried yeast
1 large onion
125g · 4oz feta or other similar
   sheep's milk cheese

500g · 1lb 2oz strong, plain
   white flour
2tsp salt
1tbsp olive or sunflower oil

Put a third of the water into a large mixing bowl and sprinkle in the yeast. Leave fresh yeast for 5 minutes and dried for 15 minutes.

Finely chop the onion and the cheese. Mix the flour and salt together.

Add the remaining water to the yeast. Add the flour mixture and then the onion and cheese. Mix together to form a dough. Turn the dough onto a floured work surface and knead it until it is smooth. Return the dough to the bowl. Cover it with a clean cloth and leave it in a warm place for 1 hour, or until it has doubled in size.

Heat the oven to 200°C/400°F/gas mark 6. Knead the dough again and form it into an oval shape about 25cm/10in long; place it on a floured baking sheet. Brush the surface with the oil and then make three diagonal slashes on the top. Leave the loaf in a warm place to prove for 20 minutes.

Bake the loaf for 35 minutes, or until the top is golden brown and it sounds hollow when tapped. Lift it onto a wire rack to cool.

PRAWN *and* BEANSHOOT BUNS

Bread does not feature very much in the Chinese diet apart from in Canton, where the speciality is the dim sum meal, eaten as a snack either in the middle of the morning or the afternoon, usually at a local dim sum restaurant. Dim sum means 'to please the heart' and the meal should be an enjoyable treat. Chinese buns are made with a soft, plain dough formed around a filling that can be either sweet or savoury, and steamed in a special bamboo steamer. The dough has no salt added, so it has a slightly sweet flavour. The recipe below makes an excellent snack or one of several dishes in a Chinese meal.

MAKES 12 BUNS

4tbsp warm water	FILLING
30g • 1oz fresh yeast or	15g • ½oz fresh root ginger
15g • ½oz dried yeast	4 spring onions
2tsp sugar	4tbsp sunflower or peanut oil
500g • 1lb 2oz strong, plain	1 garlic clove, finely chopped
white flour	125g • 4oz peeled prawns
300ml • 10fl oz warm milk	125g • 4oz bean shoots
	2tbsp soy sauce
	2tbsp dry sherry (optional)

To make the dough, put the warm water into a small bowl and sprinkle in the yeast and sugar. Leave fresh yeast for 5 minutes and dried for 15 minutes.

Put the flour into a mixing bowl and make a well in the centre. Pour in the yeast mixture and the milk and mix to a dough. Turn the dough onto a floured board and knead it until it is smooth. Return the dough to the bowl. Cover it with a clean cloth and leave it in a warm place for 1 hour to double in size. Knock the dough down firmly with your fist, cover it again and leave it for a further 30 minutes, or until it has again doubled in size.

To make the filling, peel and grate the ginger and chop the spring onions. Heat the oil in a frying pan on a high heat. Put in the ginger, spring onions and garlic and stir for 30 seconds. Add the prawns and stir for a further 30 seconds. Add the beanshoots and stir for 2 minutes or until they are wilted. Add the soy sauce and sherry and let them bubble until they are reduced by half. Take the pan from the heat and cool the contents.

Knead the dough again and cut it into 12 pieces. Roll each piece into a 10cm/4in round. Put a portion of the filling in the centre of each round. Gather up the sides of each round so they meet at the top and twist them round to secure the edges. Put the buns onto a floured work surface. Cover them with a clean cloth and leave them to prove for 30 minutes.

Bring some water to the boil under a large steamer. Put in as many buns as the steamer will take, leaving a space of about 2.5cm/1in around each one. Cover the buns and steam them for 10 minutes. Cook the rest in the same way. If the buns have to be cooked in two or more batches, put the ones cooked first on top of the ones still cooking for the last 2 minutes of cooking time, so they can all be served hot.

ANCHOVY BREAD

A sourdough type of bread flavoured with anchovies is a speciality of Provence in France. This variation is rich and well-flavoured and excellent served, unbuttered, with savoury casseroles and stews.

MAKES ONE 1KG · 2LBS 4OZ LOAF

180ml • 6fl oz warm water	*1 tsp salt*
15g • ½oz fresh yeast or 2tsp dried yeast	*2 45g • 1 ½oz tins anchovy fillets*
500g • 1lb 2oz strong, plain white flour	*60g • 2oz butter, softened*
	2 eggs, beaten

Put the water into a large mixing bowl and sprinkle in the yeast. Leave fresh yeast for 5 minutes and dried yeast for 15 minutes.

Add half the flour and all the salt. Mix to a dough. Turn the dough onto a floured work surface and knead it until it is smooth. Return it to the bowl. Cover it with plastic film and leave it in a warm place for 2 days.

Drain and mash the anchovies. Leaving the dough in the bowl, knead in the butter and then the eggs, a little at a time. It will take at least 10 minutes for them both to be incorporated. Knead in the remaining flour. Turn the dough onto a work surface and knead it until it is smooth. Return it to the bowl again, cover it with a cloth and leave it in a warm place for 1 hour, or until it has doubled in size.

Heat the oven to 200°C/400°F/gas mark 6. Knead the dough again, form it into a ball and place it on a floured baking sheet. Leave the dough in a warm place for 20 minutes to prove.

Bake the loaf for 25 minutes, or until the top is golden brown and sounds hollow when tapped. Lift it onto a wire rack to cool.

CHEESE-FILLED BUNS

These buns are based on a Russian recipe called *khachapuri*. The original recipe would have used a local sheep's milk cheese, but feta makes a good substitute. The buns are made from a plain bread dough which encloses a savoury filling of cheese. You can vary the filling if desired. The buns make ideal fare for lunch boxes and picnics.

MAKES 16 BUNS

150ml • 5fl oz warm milk	FILLING
15g • ½oz fresh yeast or 2tsp dried yeast	*185g • 6oz feta cheese, grated*
60g • 2oz butter, softened	*1 egg, beaten*
280g • 10oz strong, plain white flour	*4tbsp fresh parsley or coriander, chopped*
1tsp salt	

To make the dough, put the milk into a large mixing bowl and sprinkle in the yeast. Leave fresh yeast for 5 minutes and dried for 15 minutes.

Add the butter to the milk and yeast. Mix in the flour and salt and knead to a dough. Turn the dough onto a floured work surface and knead it until it is smooth. Return the dough to the bowl. Cover it with a clean cloth and leave it in a warm place for 1 hour, or until it has doubled in size.

To make the filling, thoroughly mix the cheese, egg and parsley together.

Heat the oven to 200°C/400°F/gas mark 6. Knead the dough again and divide it into 16 even-sized pieces. Roll each piece into a circle about 13cm/5in in diameter. Place a portion of the filling in the centre of each circle. Fold in two opposite sides of each circle to just touch in the centre. Fold in the two opposite sides in the same way. Pinch the corners to seal. Put the buns onto floured baking sheets and leave them in a warm place for 20 minutes to prove.

Bake the buns for 20 minutes, or until they are just brown. Cool them on wire racks. Either eat them warm, or cool them completely for picnics and lunch boxes.

Advertising and Packaging

For thousands of years, bread, like other goods, was sold and advertised by a variety of direct methods in the street and at fairs and markets. It was not until newspapers and magazines became widely available that advertising took on its modern form.

Ever since bread has been baked commercially, bakers have been finding ways to ensure that their products came to the public eye and commanded a good share of the market.

Up until the nineteenth century and the rise of literacy, which allowed the use of written signs, it was common to see people carrying trays of all kinds of goods through the streets, calling out to passers-by to come and sample their wares. People would come from their houses when they heard the baker's cries and buy his goods while still hot from the oven. Other things being equal, the baker who shouted loudest or had the cleverest turn of phrase would sell the most. This is the origin of the old street cries, some of which have survived as nursery rhymes, such as:

'Hot cross buns,
Hot cross buns,
One a penny,
Two a penny,
Hot cross buns.
If you have no daughters
Give them to your sons.
One a penny,
Two a penny,
Hot cross buns.'

Another method of attracting customers was for the baker to display his wares outside his bakery. People in a crowded street market or fairground would look for a loaf of bread impaled on a pole standing high above the heads of shoppers and the frames of stalls.

Towards the end of the nineteenth century, bakers began to switch from making bread by hand to making it by machine. There was then little difference between any of the standard loaves on sale, and thus began the modern push towards 'brand awareness'. As more people became literate and newspapers and magazines became readily available, advertising as we know it began, and copywriters started their never-ending search for the perfect slogan.

In Britain, for example, S. Fitton and Son, millers of Macclesfield, began to promote Hovis flour for breadmaking. Their campaign was based on the fact that their product was 'Supplied to The Queen and Royal Family'. In the patriotic days of Queen Victoria and the Empire, that was a great selling point in itself. However, their advertisements also proclaimed that: '1 1/2lb Hovis Bread is more nourishing than 1/2 lb Beef Steak', and that their bread was 'Absolutely Necessary for all growing

This nineteenth-century advertisement for Ever-Fresh Bread gives the impression that it was the choice of royalty – a sure selling point in Britain at that time.

Advertisers have always focused on the health benefits of bread. In Britain, during the early part of this century, many children were undernourished, so this claim would would have appealed to many mothers.

In the late 1800s, American companies began marketing specialty flours to home breadmakers.

children'. Hovis bread advertisements appeared in numerous magazines, and nearly every small baker and grocer in the country had a metal sign bearing the one word 'Hovis' fixed to the outside of his shop. These signs have now become collector's items and museum pieces.

In America, sliced bread was first marketed on a commercial scale in 1928, soon after the first commercial bread slicer was installed in Missouri. Before that, unsliced bread was sold commercially, but the vast majority of people bought their bread from neighbourhood grocers and door-to-door pushcart vendors. Once wrapping was introduced, a whole new area of advertising was opened up.

Initially, some bakers resisted the idea of wrapping. This was particularly true of Australian bakers, who were 'unanimously opposed . . . on the grounds of cost, uncertainty of hygienic benefit [and] total lack of public demand'. However, by 1928 three Sydney bakers were wrapping their loaves, and others soon followed.

After the Second World War, the sliced, wrapped loaf became increasingly popular, and this was a golden opportunity for manufacturers to give their loaves fancy names and eye-catching wrappers bearing distinctive logos. One of the most widely recognized trademarks in the American food industry is Miss Sunbeam, the symbol for Sunbeam bread, created in 1942 for the Quality Bakers of America. Inspired by a little girl playing in a park in New York City, the image of a sweet, blond child doubled sales in just 13 weeks and spun off into a hugely profitable industry of promotional dolls and other toys.

In Britain, there was Wonder Bread, which 'Helps Build Bodies Twelve Ways', and Taystee enriched bread, 'with wholesome good taste'. Both these advertising campaigns relied on promoting the nutritional quality of the loaves in question – and this has been the underlying theme of most bread advertisements for the last fifty years.

Promotion was not restricted to bread; manufacturers also advertised bread-making ingredients to both commercial and home bakers. In 1880, for example, the Washburn Crosby company of Minneapolis, Minnesota (the forerunner of General Mills), entered its flour in the first Millers' International Exhibition and took the gold, silver and bronze medals. From then on, the company's highest quality flour has been marketed under the Good Medal brand.

Today's consumers can choose from a vast range of ingredients and breads, and advertisers are having to become ever more creative in promoting brand awareness

Even plain, uncut loaves can be given an eye-catching wrapper that promotes the brand name and logo and also gives nutritional information.

In the 1880s, Pillsbury Best flour appeared in the United States and was heavily promoted by the family whose name it bears. The Pillsbury Man is now one of the most widely recognised promotional figures in the American bread-making

LARDY CAKE

Lardy cake is another traditional bread from rural England. When large batches of bread were made at home, a small portion of the dough was set aside to be rolled and layered with sugar, spices, dried fruit and lard. Eaten warm, it is an old-fashioned tea-time treat, moist, sweet and spicy and with the layers still visible and adding interest to the texture. Wholewheat bread gives a nostalgic, country flavour.

MAKES ONE 25CM · 10IN LOAF

plain bread dough made with
  500g · 1lb 2oz strong, plain white flour or wholewheat flour
185g · 6oz lard
125g · 4oz soft brown sugar

60g · 2oz currants
60g · 2oz raisins
1tsp ground mixed spice
GLAZE
1tbsp sugar dissolved in 1tbsp water

Make up the bread dough (see page 30) and leave it to rise for 1 hour. Heat the oven to 200°C/400°F/gas mark 6.

Knead the dough on a floured work surface. Roll it out into a rectangle about 12mm/½in thick. Spread 30g/1oz of the lard on two-thirds of the dough and fold the dough into three. Roll the dough out again and spread on a quarter of the lard that is left (35g or just over 1oz). Mix together the sugar, dried fruit and spice. Sprinkle a quarter of the mixture over the dough. Fold the dough into three. Repeat the process three times, using 35g/1oz and 15g/½ oz each of currants and raisins each time, the last time folding the dough but not rolling it out again.

Place the folded dough in a baking tin about 25 × 20cm/ 10 × 8in. (Do not use a baking sheet as the lard sometimes runs out during cooking.) Leave it in a warm place to prove for 15 minutes. Bake the loaf for 40 minutes, or until it is golden brown and sounds hollow when tapped. Brush it with the glaze and return it to the oven for 1 minute. Turn the loaf onto a wire rack to cool a little. If possible, eat it warm.

CHELSEA BUNS

Chelsea buns were first made in the early part of the nineteenth century in The Old Chelsea Bun House in the Pimlico Road in London. The proprietor was Mr Richard Hand, who ran the establishment with his family and who was known as Captain Bun. Crowds of people would travel from the city to the Bun House at weekends to taste the rich, sweet, sticky buns hot from the oven. Even King George III and Queen Charlotte were regularly seen there. The Old Chelsea Bun House burnt down in 1839, but fortunately Chelsea buns have been made ever since.

MAKES 12 BUNS

150ml · 5fl oz warm milk
30g · 1oz fresh yeast or 15g · ½oz dried yeast
655g · 1lb 5oz strong, plain white flour
½tsp salt
155g · 7oz caster sugar

4 eggs, beaten
155g · 7oz butter, softened
155g · 7oz currants
1tsp ground mixed spice
GLAZE
60g · 2oz sugar boiled with 2tbsp water

Put the milk into a small bowl and sprinkle in the yeast. Leave fresh yeast for 5 minutes and dried for 15 minutes.

Put the flour into a bowl. Mix in the salt and half the sugar. Make a well in the centre. Pour in the yeast mixture and the eggs and put in half the butter. Mix to a dough. Turn it onto a floured work surface and knead it until it is smooth. Return the dough to the bowl. Cover it with a clean cloth and leave it in a warm place for 1 hour, or until it has doubled in size.

Heat the oven to 200°C/400°F/gas mark 6. Knead the dough again and roll it into a square about 12mm/½in thick. Spread it with the remaining butter and sprinkle on half the remaining sugar. Fold the dough into three and roll it out again. Sprinkle it with the remaining sugar and all the currants and spice. Roll it up like a Swiss roll. Cut the roll into 12 slices, each 3–4cm/1 ½in thick. Place the slices close together, but not quite touching, on a floured baking sheet. Leave them for 20 minutes to prove, by which time they should be touching each other.

Bake the buns for 20 minutes, or until they are golden brown. Brush them with the prepared glaze and return them to the oven for 2 minutes for the glaze to dry. Cool the buns on wire racks, still joined together. Pull them apart just before serving.

CHAPTER THREE

FLAT BREAD

lat breads are made all over the world. Some are eaten as snacks, many are used to accompany a meal and others serve as both food and eating utensil combined. The enormous variety of textures and shapes makes for an exciting accompaniment to any meal.

FLAT BREAD

The very earliest breads were unyeasted and baked flat on a hot stone, and many flat breads are still made in the same way and enjoyed today. There are soft, flexible chapatis and tasty tortillas for wrapping around food, as well as more substantial parathas, flavoured with spice, while Sweden's knackebrod and other crispbreads go well with cheese. Adding yeast, or another raising agent, makes a thicker, puffier dough, even when it is rolled flat for baking.

Nan bread is rolled into oval shapes while pitta bread forms a handy pocket to hold food. Topped with herbs and sesame seeds and baked in rounds, flat bread becomes a favourite Middle Eastern snack called mannaeesh. Italian focaccia accompanies cheese, salads or cooked dishes and the apple and walnut crumble cake from Germany makes a hearty dessert. For a traditional English tea, nothing can beat warm, buttery crumpets and girdle scones .

From sowing to loaf, *19th century*

MANNAEESH

These breads are a variation of ones that are popular in the Lebanon. There they have a strongly flavoured topping made with large amounts of dried herbs together with sesame seeds. The smaller amounts of fresh herbs give a much milder flavour more suited to Western palates. *Mannaeesh* are eaten for breakfast, with tea or coffee, but are also excellent with soups and salads. They are soft and very light.

MAKES 10 SMALL, ROUND BREADS

300ml • 10fl oz warm water
15g • ½oz fresh yeast or
   2tsp dried yeast
2tbsp olive oil
500g • 1lb 2oz strong, plain
   white flour
½tsp salt

TOPPING

90ml • 3fl oz olive oil
4tbsp fresh thyme, chopped
4tbsp fresh marjoram, chopped
3tbsp sesame seeds

Put the water into a large mixing bowl and sprinkle in the yeast. Leave fresh yeast for 5 minutes and dried for 15 minutes. Add the oil. Stir in the flour and salt. Form the mixture into a dough. Turn it onto a floured work surface and knead it well. Return the dough to the bowl and cover it with a clean cloth. Leave it in a warm place for 1 hour, or until it has doubled in size.

Heat the oven to 230°C/450°F/gas mark 8. Mix together the topping ingredients.

Knead the dough for a second time and divide it into 10 equal pieces. Roll each piece into a flat round, about 13cm/5in in diameter. Place them on a floured work surface and leave them for 20 minutes. Cover four baking sheets in foil and put them into the oven to heat.

Spread the topping mixture evenly over each round of bread and place the rounds on the hot baking sheets. Bake for 8 minutes, or until the bread is cooked through but still soft and white. Lift them onto wire racks to cool.

BUCKWHEAT BREAD

In the Baltic States, and in Poland, buckwheat flour is used to make a dark, crumbly bread with a rich, distinctive flavour. Because buckwheat flour contains no gluten, the rising qualities of bread made with it are poor, so it is often mixed with a varying proportion of wheat flour. Buckwheat bread does not slice firmly like ordinary bread so it is often made in flat shapes to be cut into wedges. It is an excellent accompaniment to salads and hearty soups.

MAKES ONE 25CM · 10IN LOAF

360ml · 12fl oz warm water
30g · 1oz fresh or 15g · ½oz dried yeast
375g · 13oz buckwheat flour
250g · 9oz strong, plain white flour
1tsp salt
125g · 4oz lard, melted, plus extra for greasing

Put 150ml/5fl oz of the water into a small bowl and sprinkle in the yeast. Leave fresh yeast for 5 minutes and dried for 15 minutes.

In a large mixing bowl, mix the two types of flour and the salt. Make a well in the centre and pour in the melted lard. Gradually begin to mix it in and then add the yeast mixture and the remaining water. Mix to a dough and then knead it in the bowl until it is smooth. Cover the dough with a clean cloth and leave it in a warm place for 1½ hours, or until it has doubled in size.

Heat the oven to 180°C/350°F/gas mark 4. Knead the dough once again in the bowl. Press it into a greased 25cm/10in diameter tart tin with a removable base. Leave it in a warm place for 30 minutes to prove. Bake the loaf for 30 minutes, or until it sounds hollow when tapped. Very carefully lift the loaf out of the tin, using the removable base, and slide it onto a wire rack to cool. It will be very crumbly at this stage, so handle it gently. It will firm up as it cools.

DANISH CRISPBREADS

The crispbread was devised in Scandinavia where summers tend to be short and the wheat harvested early. To save work in the long, hard winters, it was ground immediately and made into breads that could be stored for a long time. Rye is by far the most widely grown grain in Denmark and so it is the principal flour in the following recipe. Eat the crispbreads simply buttered, or enjoy them with cheeses, dips, pâtés and salads.

MAKES EIGHT 25CM · 10IN OR SIXTEEN 13CM · 5IN CRISPBREADS

330ml · 11fl oz boiling water
30g · 1oz butter
185g · 6oz whole rye flour
90g · 3oz wholewheat flour
90g · 3oz plain, white cake flour
½ tsp salt

Heat the oven to 230°C/450°F/gas mark 8. Pour the water into a large mixing bowl and whisk in the butter. Mix the flours and salt together. Beat them into the water and butter, a little at a time. Use a wooden spoon at first, then knead in the final third of the flour with your hand. Turn the mixture onto a floured work surface and knead it until it is smooth.

Divide the dough into either 8 or 16 pieces. Roll large pieces into 25cm/10in rounds and smaller pieces into 13cm/5in rounds. Place the rounds on floured baking sheets and bake them for about 5 minutes, or until they are crisp but only very lightly coloured. Cool them on wire racks. If you have to cook several batches in succession because all the crispbreads will not fit into your oven, cool the trays completely between batches.

Crispbreads can be stored for future use by wrapping them in fours in a double layer of plastic film. Keep them in a cool, dry place.

Pizza and Calzone

The pizza was invented in Naples in the eighteenth century and has spread around the world, providing a complete meal in itself.

A nourishing combination of bread and savoury flavourings, a use for tomatoes when they arrived from the New World, an indication of the price of food and a way to show the colours of the Italian flag – the pizza has been all of these, but essentially it is a complete meal.

Ever since Roman times, the Italians have been fond of small, flat, savoury-topped breads. The Romans baked them on heated stones and brushed them with mixtures of olive oil, herbs and honey. Today, in the region of Romagna, small round breads, enriched with pork fat, are topped with ham, salami or local cheese and folded in half to make an easily eaten snack.

The pizza, as the rest of the world knows it today, was first devised in Naples in the eighteenth century and owes its existence to the discovery of tomatoes in the Americas. Tomatoes first arrived in Italy in the late sixteenth century, but it took some time for them to become established as a crop and for new varieties, suited to the Italian climate, to be developed. The area around Naples proved to have the perfect climate for growing tomatoes, and at harvest time they were stewed in large cooking pots to make a rich sauce to serve with meats and add to casseroles. It was very soon discovered that the sauce also made an ideal topping for the local flat bread.

Pizzas have rarely been made at home in Italy. When they first appeared, they were sold from stalls in the streets. By the nineteenth century, their fame had spread and *pizzerie* (pizza shops) had been set up all over Naples. One such shop, the *Pietro il Pizzaiolo*, became so renowned that news of it spread to Queen Margherita in Rome. She visited Naples in 1889 and went straight to the shop to try its wares. She was given three different pizzas to sample. One was topped simply with tomatoes, garlic and oil, and another with pork fat, cheese and basil, but her favourite was the one with tomatoes, mozzarella cheese and basil (the colours of the Italian flag). It was this one that became the standard Pizza Napolitana, that is still the most popular pizza today.

Italian immigrants took the pizza to the USA, where pizzeria were soon set up, but it was only relatively recently that pizzas arrived in the UK. The pizza is now available throughout most of the world.

There is an art in making a perfect pizza dough, and many Italian housewives buy either finished pizzas or the dough. The Neapolitan *pizzaioli* are able to stretch the dough so that it is almost paper thin before adding the topping.

However, it is not difficult to make a pizza yourself, including the dough, using strong white flour, yeast and water. Adding a little olive oil gives a crisper edge to the baked crust.

Basic Pizza Dough

Makes one 25cm • 10in pizza or two 18cm • 7in pizzas

250g • 9oz strong, plain white flour
15g • ½oz fresh yeast or 1tbsp dried yeast
150ml • 5fl oz warm water
1tsp salt
1tbsp olive oil

Make up the dough as for the plain bread dough on page 30, adding the olive oil with the water. Knead it and leave it to rise in the usual way. Heat the oven to 200°C/400°F/gas mark 6.
For one large pizza, roll the dough into a round about 28cm/11in in diameter. Fold over 12mm/½ in all the way round. To make individual pizzas, divide the dough into two and roll each piece to a diameter of about 20cm/8in.
Place the round on a baking sheet and put your chosen filling on top, leaving a border of about 2cm/¾in. Leave the pizza to prove for 20 minutes. Bake it for 15 minutes, or until the bread is cooked through but not too browned round the edges.
If possible, eat the pizza hot so both base and topping are the perfect texture.

Tomato Sauce for Pizza

For one 25cm • 10in or two 18cm • 7in pizzas

500g • 1lb ripe red tomatoes
2 tbsp olive oil
1 small onion, finely chopped (optional)
1 garlic clove, finely chopped (optional)

Scald, skin and chop the tomatoes. Heat the oil in a frying pan on a low heat. If you are adding onions and/or garlic, gently soften them in the oil first. Add the tomatoes and simmer, stirring frequently, for 50 minutes, or until you have a thick purée. Leave the purée to cool before spooning it over the pizza.

Pizza Napolitana

pizza dough (left)
tomato sauce (above)
175g • 6oz mozzarella cheese, thinly sliced
1tsp chopped basil or about 15 whole oregano leaves

Spread the tomato sauce over the pizza dough first. Place the slices of mozzarella over the tomato sauce and scatter the herbs over the top.

Calzone

Take some pizza dough, make it into a pocket, fill it with something tasty, deep-fry it so it is crisp and golden and you have a *calzone*.
To make *calzone*, take the basic pizza dough and divide it into two pieces. Roll each piece into a thin, 20cm/8in round. Place your chosen filling ingredients on half the round. Fold over the other half and seal the edges.
Put about 4cm/1½in olive or sunflower oil into a saucepan or casserole that will easily take the *calzone* lying flat. An oval-shaped one is ideal. Heat the oil on a high heat. (Olive oil has a relatively low flash point, so take care if using this.)
Put in the first *calzone* and fry it until the underside is golden brown, about 1½ minutes. Turn it over and brown the other side. Lift out the *calzone* with a slotted spoon or slice and put it into a shallow dish lined with kitchen paper. Cook the others in the same way and serve them as soon as possible.

83

Fillings for Calzone

Try mozzarella cheese, thin slices of prosciutto ham or salami, a mixture of ricotta, mozzarella and pecorino cheeses, or a combination of mozzarella and ham or salami. You can also spread the whole of the top of the dough with ricotta cheese before placing the other filling ingredients on top.

CHAPATIS

Chapatis have become familiar to the West through Indian restaurants. They are the traditional bread of India, made with a very fine wholewheat flour and cooked at home on a cast-iron griddle called a *tava*. Chapati flour can be bought in ethnic food shops and health food stores. If it is unavailable, use a half-and-half mixture of plain cake flour and wholewheat flour. Chapatis are simple to make, but the longer the dough is allowed to stand after mixing, the softer and more pliable the end result will be. Serve the chapatis with curry dishes. In India, they are used as an edible form of eating utensil, small pieces are torn off and wrapped around mouthfuls of food. Brush the loaves repeatedly with water as they bake.

MAKES 8 CHAPATIS

280g • 10oz chapati flour
1tsp salt

up to 200ml • 7fl oz water

Put the flour and salt into a bowl. Make a well in the centre and gradually mix in 150ml/5fl oz of the water. You need to make a smooth and elastic dough in which the flour has absorbed all the water, so check the consistency and add more water, no more than 1tbsp at a time, if you think it is necessary. Turn the dough onto a floured work surface and knead it for 5–10 minutes. Wrap it in a wet cloth and leave it in a cool place for 1–2 hours. Alternatively, refrigerate it for up to 7 hours.

When you are ready to cook, divide the dough into 8 equal-sized pieces. Roll each piece into a thin round about 25cm/10in in diameter. Once rolled, leave them separate to prevent them from sticking together.

Heat an ungreased griddle on a medium heat. Warm a dish and a clean, dry cloth. Place one chapati on the griddle and cook it until it begins to bubble. Turn the chapati over and leave it until it is cooked through; to ensure even cooking, turn it several times. Put the cloth in the heated dish and place the first chapati on it. Fold the cloth over it and keep it warm. Cook the remaining chapatis in the same way and make a pile of them as they are ready. Eat them as soon as possible.

NAN

Nan, or naan, bread is eaten in all areas of India, Pakistan, Bangladesh and Afghanistan, and there are many different types which vary according to the raising agent used and whether they are plain or made with a flavoured topping. In most cases, the liquid used for mixing is yoghurt. Nan is also made in a variety of sizes. These ones are large, like the ones you find in Afghanistan. They are soft, with a bouncy texture, and full of flavour.

MAKES THREE 25CM · 10IN OVAL BREADS

500g • 1lb 2oz strong, plain
    white flour
½tsp salt
250ml • 9fl oz thin,
    natural yoghurt
30g • 1oz fresh yeast or
    15g • ½oz dried yeast
2 eggs, beaten
90g • 3oz ghee or
    clarified butter

ALTERNATIVE TOPPINGS (THESE AMOUNTS WILL TOP 3 BREADS)
2tbsp sesame seeds
1 medium onion, finely chopped
2 garlic cloves, crushed
4tbsp chopped fresh coriander
    leaves

Put the flour and salt into a bowl and make a well in the centre. Gently warm the yoghurt to lukewarm and sprinkle in the yeast. Leave fresh yeast for 5 minutes and dried yeast for 15 minutes.

Pour the yoghurt and yeast mixture into the flour. Add the eggs and 30g/1oz of the melted *ghee*. Mix to a dough. Turn it onto a floured board and knead it until it is smooth. Return the dough to the bowl. Cover it with a clean cloth and leave it in a warm place to rise for 2 hours. It will double in size after 1 hour, but allowing such a long rising time gives a distinctive flavour.

Heat the oven to 200°C/400°F/gas mark 6. Prepare your chosen toppings, if using any. Leave the sesame seeds and chopped onion as they are. Mix the crushed garlic on its own or with the coriander leaves with the remaining melted *ghee*.

Knead the dough again and divide it into three equal pieces. Roll each piece into an oval shape, wider at one end than the other and about 25cm/10in long. Place the breads on a floured work surface for 10 minutes to prove.

Spread cooking foil over three baking sheets and heat the baking sheets and foil in the oven. Place the breads on the hot baking sheets. Either brush them thickly with *ghee* or add one of the toppings; sprinkle over the sesame seeds or chopped onion, or brush them with the *ghee* into which the garlic and coriander has been mixed.

Bake the nan for 7 minutes, or until they are just browned, lightly risen and still soft. Lift them onto clean towels to cool and serve them warm.

GIRDLE SCONES

Girdle is another term for a griddle, or a thick, round iron plate. The term originates from the northern counties of England where this method of cooking breads has remained despite changes to oven cooking. Girdle scones are best served hot, straight from the griddle, split and buttered, sandwiched back together and cut into wedges. Plain, the scones can be served with sweet or savoury spreads or, if currants are added, served with jam or preserves.

MAKES TWO 13CM · 5IN DIAMETER SCONES

350g · 12oz plain, white cake flour
1tsp salt
½tsp bicarbonate of soda
90g · 3oz lard or butter, plus extra for greasing
125g · 4oz currants (optional)
125ml · 4fl oz soured cream
up to 100ml · 3½fl oz milk

Put the flour into a mixing bowl. Add the salt and bicarbonate of soda and rub in the lard or butter. Add the currants, if using. Make a well in the centre and pour in all the soured cream. Then mix in enough milk to make a smooth, pliable dough.

Divide the dough into two and roll each piece into a round about 13cm/5in in diameter and 2cm/¾in thick.

Heat a lightly greased griddle on a low heat. Place one of the scones on the griddle and cook it for 5–7 minutes, or until it is golden brown and firm on one side. Using two fish slices, carefully turn the scone over and brown the other side.

When done, the scone should sound hollow when tapped.

Lift the scone onto a wire rack and cool for 5 minutes before splitting and buttering it. Then cook the other scone in the same way.

KNACKEBROD

Knackebrod are like semi-sweet oatcakes. In Sweden, they are the most popular type of crispbread; here they are made with a special 'hob-nail' rolling pin that makes a pattern in the dough as it is rolled. They are equally successful, however, rolled out with a normal rolling pin. Serve them with cheeses, dips and pâtés.

MAKES ABOUT 64 SMALL CRISPBREADS

60g · 2oz lard or shortening
30g · 1oz butter
60g · 2oz sugar
125g · 4oz rolled oats
185g · 6oz strong, plain white flour
1tsp salt
1tsp bicarbonate of soda
180ml · 6fl oz cultured buttermilk (or milk in which you have dissolved ½tsp cream of tartar)

Cream together the lard or shortening, butter and sugar in a large mixing bowl. Mix together the oats, flour, salt and bicarbonate of soda. Alternatively, add the flour mixture and the buttermilk to the fats and sugar, working with your hand towards the end to make a stiff dough. With the dough still in the bowl, form it into a ball; put it into the refrigerator for 30 minutes.

Heat the oven to 170°C/325°F/gas mark 3. Divide the dough into four pieces and refrigerate three of them. Place the remaining ball of dough on a floured baking sheet and roll it out into a 30cm/12in square. Prick it all over with a fork. Using a pastry wheel or knife, score the large square into 16 small squares. Do the same with the other pieces of dough.

Bake the crispbreads for 15–20 minutes, or until they are crisp and golden. Cool them for 2 minutes on the baking sheets and then transfer them to wire racks to cool. Store the crispbreads in an airtight tin.

Kachoris and Puris

The Indian city of Varanasi (Benares) in Uttar Pradesh is one of the holiest cities for the Hindu people. Through it flows the sacred Ganges, and pilgrims come from all over the country to visit it, particularly at Diwali, the Festival of Lights.

Many of these pilgrims make their way to Kachori Gulley, the Lane of Fried Breads. Here they can buy freshly cooked, small rounds of bread, fried until they are soft in the middle and golden and crisp on the outside. It is said in the city that it takes many years to perfect the art of making the perfect kachori. *They should be so light that if 25 were stacked on a plate and you dropped a coin on top, you could still hear the sound of the coin hitting the plate.*

When a kachori *is stuffed with a savoury filling, it becomes a substantial snack called a* puri. *Stuffings include spiced chick-peas or lentils, fenugreek leaves, potatoes stewed with ginger and cumin, and a spiced combination of potatoes and pumpkin. Hindus are vegetarians and these foods make a nutritious contribution to their diet.*

87

TORTILLAS

Tortillas are prepared by hand in homes all over Mexico and there are also tortilla factories and tortilla shops that sell them both part-prepared and fully cooked. They are Mexico's national bread, and the name comes from the Spanish word for 'little cakes'. In Mexico, tortillas are made from *masa*, a paste produced by soaking sweetcorn kernels in a solution of lime and grinding them when wet. *Masa* can be bought fresh in Mexico and the United States but it is not available in Europe. However, specialist food shops sell a flour called *masa harina* or dried *masa*. Like chapatis, tortillas are both food and eating utensils.

MAKES 12 TORTILLAS

280g • 10oz masa harina   *300ml • 10fl oz warm water*

Put the *masa harina* into a bowl. Add the water, a little at a time, and gradually mix it into the flour with your hand to make a dough that is moist enough to roll without pieces crumbling away. Form the dough into a ball and cover it with a clean cloth. Leave it at room temperature for 30 minutes.

Divide the dough into 12 equal-sized pieces. Place one piece of dough on your left palm and begin to pat it with your right. Turn it round a little and pat it from hand to hand, gently pushing the edges over your palm to spread the dough into a 15cm/6in round. This is the traditional Mexican way. Alternatively, if you can't get the knack, roll out the balls of dough between two pieces of plastic film.

Heat an ungreased griddle over a low heat. Warm a large plate or dish and have ready a clean, dry cloth. Place a tortilla on the griddle and cook it for about 1 minute each side, or until it is cooked through and both sides look dry, speckled and brown. Place the warmed cloth on the plate. Put the tortilla onto it and cover it with the sides of the cloth. Cook the others in the same way and make a pile as they are cooked. Serve them warm.

PITTA BREAD

In the Middle East, the word for bread is *khubz*, and what has become known as pitta bread in the West is *khubz Arabi* or Arabian bread. In Armenia it is called *pideh* (whence the word pitta comes), and here it is made with wholewheat flour. The pitta, or pita, is probably the most popular bread in the Middle East and it was being made in Babylon and Assyria in Biblical times. Pitta bread is made from a plain bread dough. It is the cooking method that produces the characteristic 'pocket'. An opened pitta bread makes a convenient container for many types of Middle Eastern food.

MAKES 10 PITTA BREADS

plain bread dough made with   wholewheat flour or a
500g • 1lb 2oz strong, plain   mixture of both
white flour

Make the dough in the usual way (page 30) and leave it in a warm place to rise for 1 hour.

Heat the oven to 230°C/450°F/gas mark 8. Knead the dough for the second time and divide it into 10 pieces. Roll each piece into an oval of about 13 × 20cm/5 × 8in. Place the pieces on a floured work surface and cover them with a clean cloth. Leave them to prove for 20 minutes.

Flour as many baking sheets as you will need to take all the breads and put them into the oven for 5 minutes to become hot. Putting the breads on hot tins in a hot oven will mean that they cook both sides at once and this will make the pockets form. Place the breads on the hot baking sheets and put them into the oven for 15 minutes, or until they are only just beginning to brown.

Wrap the breads in a clean cloth to cool slightly, then eat them warm. Alternatively, let them cool completely and reheat them under a grill when needed.

88

Parathas

Parathas are more substantial than chapatis as they are slightly thicker and made with milk and clarified butter called *ghee*. A vegetable *ghee* can also be used. *Parathas* are eaten alongside curry dishes rather than being used to wrap around mouthfuls of food.

MAKES 6 PARATHAS

280g • 10oz chapati flour	*100ml • 3½fl oz water*
½tsp salt	*100ml • 3½fl oz milk*
1tsp cumin seeds, optional	*125g • 4oz* ghee *or clarified butter, melted*

Put the flour, salt and cumin seeds into a bowl. Mix together the water and milk. Mix them into the flour, a little at a time, to make a soft, pliable dough. Turn the dough onto a floured work surface and knead it for 5 minutes. Wrap it in a wet cloth and leave it in a cool place for 1–2 hours, or in the refrigerator for up to 7 hours.

When you are ready to cook, divide the dough into 6 equal pieces and roll each one into a flat round about 15cm/6in in diameter. Brush the top surface with the melted *ghee*. Gather up the sides of the circle of dough and twist them together in the centre to form a pouch shape. Turn the dough over, twisted side down, and roll it out to a diameter of about 18cm/7in. Leave the rounds separate as they are prepared.

Warm a dish and a clean, dry cloth. Heat a griddle on a medium heat and brush it with *ghee*. Place a *paratha* on the griddle and cook it until the top begins to look as though it is drying, about 2 minutes. Brush the *paratha* with a little *ghee* and cook it until the underside is speckled brown, about 1 minute more. Turn the *paratha* over and cook it until the second side is speckled and the dough is cooked through.

Put the cloth in the heated dish and place the first *paratha* on it. Fold the cloth over it and keep it warm. Cook the remaining *parathas* in the same way, making a pile as they are cooked. Eat them as soon as possible.

Spiced Parathas

Divide the *ghee* or clarified butter into two portions, one for the initial brushing when the *parathas* are rolled, and the other for cooking. Use the cumin seeds in the recipe above. Add ½tsp ground turmeric and ½tsp ground coriander to the *ghee* for brushing. The spices can be varied according to taste, for example, replace the turmeric and coriander with 1tsp *garam masala* and a pinch of cayenne pepper. Cook as above.

Stuffed Parathas

Parathas can be stuffed with spiced, cooked mixtures of vegetables, lentils or meat. The most popular filling is made from grated raw mooli, or white radish. Grate about 90g/3oz of the radish and mix it with 1 finely chopped fresh green chilli, ½tsp ground ginger and ½tsp ground coriander. Leave the mixture for 1 hour before using. To stuff p*arathas* with any chosen mixture, put 1–2tsp of the stuffing into the centre of the circle of dough after the first rolling. Bring the edges of the dough up around the filling and make the pouch shape as above. Then turn it and roll out as for plain p*arathas*, so that the stuffing is spread inside the dough. Cook as above.

FOCACCIA

Focaccia is a soft Italian flat bread, about 2.5cm/1in thick, which was traditionally baked in large, round copper baking tins in a brick oven. In its simplest form, it is either baked plain or topped with a liberal sprinkling of salt and several tablespoons of olive oil, but there are many regional variations, both savoury and sweet. Focaccia is a favourite outdoor food, popular for both barbecues and picnics, and it is also served with cheese and with first courses.

MAKES ONE 25CM · 10IN LOAF

250ml · 9fl oz warm water	*3tbsp olive oil*
15g · ½ oz fresh yeast or	*2tsp salt*
2tsp dried yeast	TOPPING
440g · 15oz strong, plain	*3tbsp olive oil*
white flour	*1tsp salt*

Put the water into a large mixing bowl and sprinkle in the yeast. Leave fresh yeast for 5 minutes and dried for 15 minutes.

Stir in the flour, oil and salt. Form the mixture into a smooth dough. Turn it onto a floured work surface and knead it well. Return the dough to the bowl and cover it with a clean cloth. Leave it in a warm place for 1 hour, or until it has doubled in size.

Heat the oven to 200°C/400°F/gas mark 6. Knead the dough again and roll it into a 25cm/10in round. Put it into a shallow, 25cm/10in square baking tin and leave it in a warm place for 30 minutes to prove. Dimple the top of the loaf with your fingertips. Pour the oil and sprinkle the salt evenly over the top.

Bake the loaf for 20–25 minutes, or until it is golden brown. Lift it onto a wire rack to cool.

APPLE *and* WALNUT CRUMBLE CAKE

This is based on a German favourite called *Streuselkuchen*, which means 'crumble cake'. It is a combination of sliced apples and chopped walnuts sandwiched between a light, sweet, yeasted base and a crunchy crumble topping. It is delicious both served warm as a dessert and cold and sliced with morning coffee or afternoon tea.

MAKES ONE 28 X 43CM · 11 X 17IN LOAF

4tbsp warm water
15g · ¹/₂oz fresh yeast or 2 tsp dried yeast
150ml · 5fl oz warm milk
grated rind ¹/₂ lemon
75g · 2¹/₂oz sugar
1 egg
2 egg yolks
315g · 10oz strong, plain white flour
105g · 3¹/₂oz butter, cut into small pieces and softened

GLAZE
125g · 4 oz plain, white cake flour
1tsp ground cinnamon
155g · 5oz butter, cut into small pieces and softened
90g · 3oz sugar
2 medium dessert apples
60g · 2oz shelled walnuts, finely chopped

Pour the water into a small mixing bowl and sprinkle in the yeast. Leave fresh yeast for 5 minutes and dried yeast for 15 minutes. Then stir in the milk and lemon rind.

In a large mixing bowl, beat together the sugar, egg and egg yolks. Stir in the yeast and milk mixture. Gradually add the flour and beat with a wooden spoon to make a soft dough. Turn the dough onto a floured work surface and knead it until it is smooth. Return the dough to the bowl. Cover it with a clean cloth and leave it to rise for 1 hour, or until it has doubled in size.

Heat the oven to 190°C/370°F/gas mark 5. Butter a 28 × 43cm/11 × 17in Swiss roll tin.

To make the topping, put the flour into a bowl with half the cinnamon and rub in 105g/3 ½oz of the butter and all the sugar. Peel and slice the apples. Melt the remaining butter. Knead the risen dough and roll it out to fit the inside of the Swiss roll tin. Place it in the tin. Arrange a layer of apples over the dough and sprinkle them with the walnuts and the remaining cinnamon. Cover the apples with the crumble mixture and sprinkle the melted butter over the top.

Leave the cake to rest in a warm place for 10 minutes. Bake it for 45 minutes or until the top is crunchy and the base cooked through. Leave it to cool slightly in the tin before cutting it into squares. Serve it warm or cold.

CRUMPETS

Crumpets are a well-loved English tea-time treat. They are cooked on a griddle, cooled and then toasted. Because they are made from a fairly liquid batter, crumpets are made in removable metal crumpet rings. You need only two rings as they are slipped off as the crumpets are cooking. The inside of home-made crumpets is light and airy and the tops fairly smooth. Once toasted, serve them hot and buttered.

MAKES 8 CRUMPETS

300ml • 10fl oz warm milk	*250g • 9oz strong, plain*
15g • ½oz fresh yeast or	*white flour*
2tsp dried yeast	*1tsp salt*
30g • 1oz butter, softened, plus	*1 egg, beaten*
extra for greasing	

Put half the milk into a small bowl and sprinkle in the yeast. Leave fresh yeast for 5 minutes and dried yeast for 15 minutes. Dissolve the butter in the remaining milk.

Put the flour and salt into a large mixing bowl and make a well in the centre. With a wooden spoon, beat in the yeast, the milk and butter mixture and the egg to make a thick batter. Cover the batter with a clean cloth and leave it in a warm place for 1 hour, or until it is light and bubbly.

Grease a cast-iron griddle and warm it over a low heat. Lightly grease the crumpet rings and put them on the griddle. Spoon 2tbsp batter into each ring. Cook for about 3 minutes until the sides are firm and the underside firm and browned. Using a palette knife, slip the rings off the crumpets (do not touch the rings with your bare hands – they will be hot!). Turn the crumpets over and cook the second side. Start another two crumpets alongside the first, using the same rings, cleaned if necessary. During the cooking, re-grease the griddle if it becomes dry.

When the first two crumpets are done, lift them onto a wire rack to cool. To serve, toast the crumpets on each side so the outsides become firm and dry, and then butter them.

Injera

What the chapati is to Indian meals, and the tortilla to Mexican, the injera *is to Ethiopian cooking.*

Injera *are larger than either chapatis or tortillas, about 37cm/17in across, round and very thin. They are made of* teff *flour, which is ground from the finest and most delicate member of the millet family.*

Teff *flour and water are combined to make enough batter for about 30 flat breads, and then left to ferment for three to four days.* Injera *are cooked on a large, ceramic griddle, which is first heated over a wood fire. The first batch of batter is poured in a spiral fashion, starting from the outside. Unlike most flat breads, the* injera *is covered while it is cooking with a domed lid sealed at the edges with a damp rag. Each* injera *is cooked individually, taking only a few minutes. Most families make enough to last them several days.*

Because of the long fermenting time, injera *have a slightly sour flavour. They are often used as both utensil and accompaniment when eaten with a spicy stew called a* wat.

CHAPTER FOUR

QUICK BREADS

There are many bread recipes from around the world that take very little time to prepare. Take a break from a busy schedule to refresh and treat yourself with a tasty and nourishing snack. Rewarding and easy to make, these aptly named quick breads will soon become firm favourites.

Quick Breads

When baking powder and bicarbonate of soda first came into use in the nineteenth century, they opened up the way to making light, risen breads without having to wait for the dough to rise. Previously, the bread-maker had to wait for the starter, or flour and water batter, to ferment; and the rising time was slow as leavening relied exclusively on yeasts naturally present in the atmosphere. Versatile quick breads can be sweet or savoury; they can be cooked on a griddle, baked in the oven or steamed in a basin.

Quick breads are made in many parts of the world. Some, such as the round, flat roti from the Caribbean, are plain and intended to be served with savoury foods. Also plain is soda bread, which is popular in both Northern Ireland and the Irish Republic. Soda bread is a round, risen bread, equally good served with cheese or preserves; it can also be flavoured with herbs, spices, dried fruits and savoury ingredients. The recipe for Walnut Soda Bread shows just how versatile it can be.

There are recipes for tea breads from many parts of the world. These are not as rich as a cake but are lighter and sweeter than bread, and can be served plain or buttered to accompany afternoon tea or coffee. Dutch Gingerbread is golden and chewy, West Indian Coconut Bread tastes of the Caribbean and Dark Speckled Tea Bread is dense with tea-soaked fruit.

Une boulangerie, *Jean Colombes a Bourges 15th century*

97

AMERICAN MUFFINS

American muffins are made with baking powder and, in shape and texture, are more like cakes than the yeasted, griddle-cooked English muffin. They have been popular in the United States for most of the twentieth century and many American housewives have their own favourite sweet or savoury flavourings, which include chocolate chip, banana, raisin, nut, ketchup, pickle, cheese, bacon and pepper relish.

This is the basic recipe. It uses a mixture of two types of flour, but either one can be used alone.

MAKES 10 MUFFINS

125g • 4oz plain white cake
*   flour*
125g • 4oz wholewheat flour
1tsp salt
2tsp baking powder
2tbsp sugar (white or
*   muscovado, according*
*   to taste)*
250ml • 9fl oz milk
1 egg, beaten
45g • 1 1/2oz shortening, melted

Heat the oven to 200°C/400°F/gas mark 6. Put the two types of flour into a bowl. Add the salt, baking powder and sugar. Make a well in the centre and beat in the milk, egg and shortening to make a thick batter. Put 10 muffin cases into cake or muffin pans. Half fill them with the mixture. Bake the muffins for 20 minutes, or until they are risen and cooked through. Lift the muffins onto a wire rack to cool.

Prayer

That he may bring food out of the earth, and
wine that maketh the heart of man: and oil to
make him a cheerful countenance, and bread to
strengthen man's heart.

PRAYER BOOK

POTATO SCONES

Potato scones are a traditional English tea-time treat from Lancashire. They are also popular in parts of the United States and Canada. Potato scones can be cooked on a griddle for a softer texture or on a baking sheet in the oven for a firmer finish. Serve the scones warm and buttered, with preserves or with cheese, or use them to accompany a cooked dish such as a casserole or stew. Any leftovers can be split and toasted and enjoyed with a cup of tea.

MAKES ABOUT 15 SCONES

375g • 10oz potatoes
60g • 2oz butter, cut into small
*   pieces and softened*
4tbsp full cream milk
185g • 6oz plain cake flour or
*   wholewheat flour*
1/4tsp salt
1/2tsp bicarbonate of soda

Either heat an oven to 200°C/400°F/gas mark 6 or lightly grease a griddle.

Boil the potatoes in their skins until they are tender. This will give the scones a better flavour and texture. Drain them and peel them while they are still warm, and push them through a sieve into a mixing bowl. Beat in the butter and milk until thoroughly incorporated.

Mix the flour with the salt and bicarbonate of soda. Using a wooden spoon at first and then your hand, gradually work the flour into the potatoes to make a manageable dough. Potatoes vary in texture. If you find the dough getting very stiff before all the flour is added, there may be no need to add it all. If your dough is still quite moist after incorporating all the flour, you may need to add a very little more flour, a tablespoon at a time.

Turn the dough onto a floured work surface and roll it out to a thickness of about 12mm/1/2in. Stamp it into 6cm/2 1/2in rounds with a biscuit cutter. Leave the scones to rest in a warm place for 15 minutes.

If you are using the oven, place the scones on a lightly floured baking sheet and bake them for 15 minutes, or until they are golden brown. If you are using the griddle, heat it over a low heat. Cook the scones on the griddle for about 7 minutes on each side, or until they are golden brown and cooked through.

ORANGE *and* APRICOT TEA BREAD

Fruity tea breads made with wholewheat flour are popular in Australia and New Zealand. In the following recipe, dried apricots are used to give texture and flavour and also to act as a sugar substitute. A microwave and a food processor will speed up the soaking and mixing times quite considerably, though they are not necessary.

MAKES ONE 500G · 1LB LOAF

185g · 6oz whole dried apricots	*100ml · 3½fl oz milk*
300ml · 10fl oz pure orange juice	*280g · 10oz wholemeal flour*
	1tsp baking powder
1 egg	*¼tsp bicarbonate of soda*
4tbsp sunflower oil	*grated rind 1 medium orange*

Soak the apricots in the orange juice overnight. Or, alternatively, put the apricots and orange juice into a bowl and microwave them on full power for 2 minutes. Leave them to soak for a further 10 minutes.

Drain the apricots, reserving the juice. Chop half of them. Put the rest into a food processor with 125ml/4 fl oz of the reserved juice, and work them to a purée. Add the egg, sunflower oil and milk and work to a smooth, thick liquid. Put in the flour, baking powder, bicarbonate of soda and orange rind, and process to make a smooth mixture. Add the chopped apricots and mix them in, processing in one or two quick bursts, to keep the apricots in pieces.

If you are not using a food processor, purée half the apricots in a blender. Put the flour into a bowl and add the baking powder, bicarbonate of soda and orange rind. Make a well in the centre and add the puréed apricots, egg and sunflower oil. Begin to beat in flour from the sides of the well and gradually beat in the milk to make a smooth mixture. Fold in the chopped apricots.

Put the mixture into a greased 500g/1lb 2oz loaf tin. Bake for 40 minutes or until the top of the loaf is brown and a skewer inserted in the centre comes out clean. Turn the loaf onto a wire rack to cool.

GOLDEN SYRUP TEA BREAD

This golden-coloured loaf is light and moist. Serve it sliced, either plain or buttered, as a mid-morning snack or with afternoon tea. Being sweet but not sticky, it also makes excellent lunch box fare.

MAKES ONE 500G · 1LB 2OZ LOAF

280g · 10oz plain white cake flour
½tsp bicarbonate of soda
¼ nutmeg, grated
60g · 2oz demerara sugar
4tbsp golden syrup
1 egg, beaten
150ml · 5fl oz milk
90g · 3oz raisins

Heat the oven to 180°C/350°F/gas mark 4. Put the flour into a bowl, add the bicarbonate of soda and the nutmeg. Mix them lightly together and make a well in the centre.

Put the sugar and golden syrup into a saucepan and melt them together over a low heat. Pour them into the well in the flour. Pour in the egg and milk and gradually beat together to make a fairly thick smooth mixture. Fold in the raisins.

Put the mixture into a greased 500g/1lb 2oz loaf tin. Bake the loaf for 50 minutes, or until the top is golden brown and a skewer inserted in the centre comes out clean. Turn the loaf onto a wire rack to cool.

DUTCH GINGERBREAD

The Dutch have a sweet tooth, and Dutch Gingerbread has a firm, brown outer crust and a golden, spicy, very sweet, springy crumb. In the 1930s Countess Morphy described it as 'one of the great national Dutch cakes or "sweet" breads'. Serve it plain or buttered.

MAKES ONE 1KG · 2LBS 4OZ LOAF

560g · 1lb 2oz plain white cake flour
3tsp baking powder
105g · 3 ½oz dark muscovado sugar
1tsp ground ginger
1tsp ground cinnamon
1tsp anise seeds
½tsp ground nutmeg
560g · 1lb 2oz golden syrup
150ml · 5fl oz milk

Heat the oven to 170°C/325°F/gas mark 3. Put the flour into a bowl and add the baking powder, sugar and spices. Mix them together with your fingers. Make a well in the centre and add the golden syrup. Put your golden syrup tin on the side pan and adjust by adding or subtracting syrup until you have the correct weight. Using a wooden spoon, begin to beat the syrup into the flour. Using a wooden spoon at first and then your hand, mix in the milk a little at a time until the mixture has a soft, dropping consistency.

Put the mixture into a greased 1kg/2lbs 4oz bread tin and smooth the top. Bake the loaf for 1 hour, or until the top is golden brown and a skewer inserted in the centre comes out clean. Turn the loaf onto a wire rack to cool.

101

Through the Looking-Glass

'A loaf of bread,' the Walrus said,
'Is what we chiefly need:
Pepper and vinegar besides
Are very good indeed –
Now if you're ready, Oysters dear,
We can begin to feed.'

LEWIS CARROLL, 1832–1898

Corn Breads

Corn bread is made from maize flour and features widely in American country cooking. It is delicious with stews, bean dishes or soup, or can be eaten on its own with butter or jam.

Towards the end of the fifteenth century, the Spaniards and the Portuguese discovered, in what is now Cuba, small fields of a tall, waving plant which the locals called by a name that sounded like 'may-ees'. Since then, this crop has become a staple in many parts of the world.

Maize, as the Europeans first termed it, yielded large husks of pea-sized grains which formed the staple diet of the islanders. The yields were large, far larger than from the same area planted with wheat, and the plant was well-suited to the hot, dry climate. It was the perfect food for both land and people, and the newcomers were quick to realise its worth. The Europeans called it 'corn', which was their word for all food grains. To distinguish it from the corn at home, it was termed 'Indian corn' or 'sweetcorn'.

Maize is still grown in the West Indies, where it was first discovered, and there it is a frequent ingredient in sweet tea breads. It was also taken back to Europe in the sixteenth century. It was unloaded at Rialto in Venice and was soon made into polenta, which is still one of the staple foods of the area. Polenta is a thick porridge that is first boiled and then set in a tin.

It can then be eaten immediately or can be baked or deep fried to give it a golden, crisp outside.

Maize also found its way back to Portugal and there it is made into a yeasted bread called *broa* whose crumbly texture and strong corn flavour make it an excellent accompaniment to hearty spiced soups and main dishes.

The Mexicans and the Peruvians had eaten corn for hundreds of years. They had developed it from a small, coarse grass and produced hundreds of varieties for different climates and altitudes, varying in colour, size and ease of cooking. In Mexico the tortilla made from corn was, and in some areas still is, served at every meal.

Seventeenth-century settlers found the crop much farther north in the American heartland, and when their own European wheat crops failed, owing mainly to an unfamiliar climate, they learned from the native Indians how to grow and how to survive on maize.

The flour produced from maize is coarse and golden yellow. Pioneers pushing back the European frontiers of America found it convenient to carry and easy to make into quick-cooking cakes and breads over camp

Corn Pone

Makes 8 small cakes

250g • 8oz cornmeal
1tsp salt
1tsp bicarbonate of soda
30g • 1oz lard or shortening
150ml • 5fl oz boiling water
150ml • 5fl oz cultured buttermilk (or milk soured with
½tsp cream of tartar)

Heat the oven to 180°C/350°F/gas mark 4. Put the cornmeal, salt and bicarbonate of soda into a mixing bowl and rub in the lard or shortening. Make a well in the centre. Pour in the boiling water, stirring in the cornmeal from the sides of the well. Add enough of the buttermilk to make a soft, pliable dough. Divide the dough into eight pieces and form each one into a round, flat cake. Put them onto a floured baking sheet and bake them for 20 minutes, or until the edges are brown. Eat them hot and buttered.

Corn pone was once cooked over the camp fires of the American pioneers. The small cakes are nourishing, quickly cooked and convenient to carry.

fires. The earliest corn breads consisted of cornmeal mixed to a dough or paste with water. Small cakes were cooked over hot ashes in a frying pan with legs, called a spider, or in makeshift ovens.

Eventually, the new settlers came to enjoy Indian corn. At first they had to eat it or starve, but even when the vast wheatlands were eventually established, corn was still grown on a large scale. Hundreds of new varieties were developed and the old corn bread recipes were still used when travelling had ceased and new houses were built. Corn bread now epitomises American country cooking.

One of the simplest corn breads is corn *pone*. The name came originally from the Indian *apone*, meaning cakes made with cornmeal and water that were cooked in the ashes. These were quickly copied by the settlers and called *pone* or ash cakes. They were cooked either on a spider or on a hoe held over the flames, when they were called hoe cakes. The recipe on the left comes from the early nineteenth century, when bicarbonate of soda became available as a raising agent.

Johnny Cake is another corn bread made by pioneers. A variety of ingredients, such as sugar or molasses, can be added, and the amount of milk or water used varies with different recipes, but the bread is always baked in a flat tin, either in the oven, in a spider or on a griddle.

Johnny Cake with Molasses

Makes one 25x20cm • 10x8in cake

175g • 6oz cornmeal
250g • 8oz plain flour
2tsp baking powder
1tsp salt
1tbsp molasses
90g • 3oz lard or shortening
500ml • 16fl oz milk, or half milk and half water

Heat the oven to 180°C/350°F/gas mark 4. Put the cornmeal, flour, baking powder and salt into a mixing bowl and rub in the molasses and lard or shortening. Make a well in the centre and gradually beat in the milk to make a thick batter. Pour the batter into a greased, 25 x 20cm/10 x 8in baking tin. Bake the cake for 30 minutes, or until it is golden brown on top and a skewer inserted into the centre comes out clean. Turn it onto a wire rack and eat it hot.

The name may come from 'journey cake', meaning that it was cooked by the side of the western trail. Or it may be a corruption of the name of the Shawnee Indian tribe who may have been responsible for teaching the early settlers how to make corn bread. No one really knows. Johnny Cake should be eaten hot and buttered. It makes an excellent accompaniment to savoury stews, bean dishes and soups but is equally good simply spread with jam.

ROTI

Roti is a Caribbean flat bread, descended from the chapatis and *puris* that were first introduced to the area by settlers from the Indian continent. *Rotis* are large and thin, baked quickly on a griddle and traditionally served with curries. For the local carnival in Port of Spain, Trinidad, the Indian population prepares enormous mounds of *rotis* and fills them to order with a selection of curries and spiced meats and pulses. Like so many of the flat breads, *rotis* act as both food and food holder.

MAKES 4 ROTIS

250g • 9oz plain white cake flour	*150ml • 5fl oz cold water*
1tsp baking powder	*90g • 3oz ghee, melted*
1tsp salt	*(unsalted butter may be used*
45g • 1 ½oz butter	*instead)*

Put the flour into a bowl. Add the baking powder and salt and rub in the butter. Make a well in the centre and pour in the water. Mix to a soft, pliable dough. Turn the dough onto a floured work surface and knead it until it is smooth. Return it to the bowl, cover it with a clean cloth and let it rest in a warm place for 30 minutes.

Knead the dough again and divide it into four equal pieces. Roll each piece into a 25cm/10in round. Fold the round in half and then half again. Roll the folded pieces of dough into rounds again, shaping the rounds using your hands and the rolling pin.

Heat an ungreased griddle on a medium heat. Warm a dish and have ready a clean, dry cloth. Place one *roti* on the griddle and cook it for about 1 minute until it is dry but not coloured on the underside. Turn it over and brush the top with melted *ghee*. Cook for another 2 minutes, then brush on more *ghee* and continue to cook for 1 minute more. The top should be bubbling and sizzling. Turn the *roti* over again and finish cooking the first side for about 2 minutes, or until it is brown and crisp. The *roti* should be cooked through but still pliable. If it is too crisp, place it on a work surface and bang it with a rolling pin or wooden mallet to break up and flake the outside.

Place the cloth in the heated dish and place the first *roti* on it. Fold the cloth over it to keep it warm. Cook the remaining *rotis* in the same way, adding them to the dish as they are ready.

WEST INDIAN COCONUT BREAD

Sweet breads, raised with bicarbonate of soda, are popular in the West Indies. There they make the most of a mixture of flours, using wheat flour, maize, cassava, breadfruit and banana flours. Local ingredients such as limes and coconuts are also found in these breads. The recipe below makes a moist loaf, with a rich coconut flavour. Serve it sliced, with tea or coffee.

MAKES ONE 1KG • 2LBS 4OZ LOAF

1 small coconut	*½tsp salt*
185g • 6oz plain white cake flour	*125g • 4oz sugar*
60g • 2oz cornmeal	*125g • 4oz unsalted butter, melted*
2tsp baking powder	*100ml • 3½fl oz evaporated milk*
½tsp ground cinnamon	
½tsp ground nutmeg	*45g • 1 ½oz raisins*
½tsp ground cloves	*45g • 1 ½oz sultanas*
grated rind 1 lime	

Heat the oven to 180°C/350°F/gas mark 4. Use a skewer to pierce through the two 'eyes' of the coconut and pour the liquid from the inside into a jug. Reserve 90ml/3fl oz coconut water. Using a heavy hammer, break open the coconut. Remove the white flesh and peel away the brown rind using a potato peeler. Grate the flesh, either by hand or using a food processor.

Put the flours and baking powder into a bowl. Add the spices, lime rind, salt and sugar and mix together. Mix in the grated coconut. Make a well in the centre and add the butter. Gradually beat in the coconut water and the evaporated milk until the mixture has a soft, dropping consistency. Mix in the raisins and sultanas.

Put the mixture into a greased 1kg/2lbs 4oz loaf tin. Bake the bread for 40 minutes, or until it is golden brown and a skewer inserted in the centre comes out clean. Turn the loaf onto a wire rack to cool.

STEAMED BROWN BREAD

Steamed bread, made with a mixture of flours, is said to have originated around Boston, New England, and also around the St Lawrence River in Canada. There is an Australian version as well, cooked in a billycan, called Brown Billy Loaf. The recipe below contains cornmeal, plain white flour and wholewheat flour. For a fuller flavour, substitute rye flour for the white.

Steamed brown bread is quick to mix but has a very long cooking time.

In the United States the bread is served hot with baked beans. It can also be cooled, sliced and buttered and eaten like ordinary bread.

MAKES ONE 375G · 12OZ LOAF

60g • 2oz cornmeal
60g • 2oz plain white cake flour
60g • 2oz wholewheat flour
½tsp salt
½tsp bicarbonate of soda
2tbsp molasses or treacle
250ml • 9fl oz cultured buttermilk, natural yoghurt, soured milk or plain milk in which you have dissolved 1tsp cream of tartar
60g • 2oz raisins (optional)

Put the different flours into a bowl, add the salt and bicarbonate of soda and mix them together. Make a well in the centre, and add the molasses. Gradually stir in the liquid to make a thick batter. Mix in the raisins, if using.

Pour the batter into a greased 600ml/1pt pudding basin. Cover the basin with a circle of greaseproof paper and then a circle of foil, both about 5cm/2in larger than the top of the basin. Tie them down with string, making a handle with a couple of loops for easy lifting.

Bring a large pan of water to the boil and place a trivet in the bottom. Lower the basin onto the trivet. Cover the pan and boil the bread for 3 hours, topping up the water, with boiling water from the kettle, when necessary. Do not allow the pan to boil dry.

Lift out the basin and turn out the bread. Serve it sliced hot with baked beans or a spicy casserole, or cooled, sliced and buttered.

Della Lutes

Della Lutes was brought up in a farmhouse in South Michigan in the USA in the 1880s and 1890s. In 1938, in England, she published a book about her memories called The Country Kitchen. *It is about 'Lijer and 'Miry, her father and mother, and their farmworkers Adelaide and Big Jim. It is written through the eyes of a child who watched with fascination the growing, harvesting and preparation of food. The centre of her world was the farmhouse kitchen, where, among other things, she helped her mother bake bread:*

'In the days when men wrested an entire living from the soil, there was little talk about dieting, and little need of it... They ate strong food, and bread was believed to be the staff of life...

'We ate meat and potatoes and pancakes. We drank quantities of milk, ate acres of bread, consumed butter by the pound, and we also ate doughnuts and cookies by the dozen. My pleasantest memory is of breakfast in a nice warm kitchen on a cold morning, with my little glass mug of milk, a huge slice of bread all buttered at once, some little pancakes cooked just for me, and my eye on the cookie plate.'

For the New Year celebrations, 'the breads were given a fair start the previous evening and then baked on the morning before the arrival of the guests. Yeast bread, salt-risin' bread, and "riz" biscuits, filling the large, sunny old kitchen with a warm, crusty fragrance which, mingled with that of roasting meat and spices released from fruity jars, teased the appetite almost beyond endurance.'

DARK SPECKLED TEA BREAD

Dark tea breads, densely speckled with dried fruits, are popular in the British Isles. Make the fruits moist and plump by soaking them in tea. Serve this delicious loaf sliced and generously buttered.

MAKES ONE 1KG · 2LBS 4OZ LOAF

185g · 6oz raisins
185g · 6oz sultanas
560ml · 18fl oz hot black tea
280g · 10oz wholemeal flour
280g · 10oz plain white cake flour
2tsp bicarbonate of soda
1tsp salt
1tsp ground mixed spice
125g · 4oz butter or lard
60g · 2oz dark muscovado sugar
1 egg, beaten
1tbsp molasses or treacle
150ml · 5fl oz natural yoghurt

Put the raisins and sultanas into a bowl and pour on the tea. Leave them for at least 4 hours. Drain the fruits and reserve the tea.

Heat the oven to 180°C/350°F/gas mark 4. Put the two sorts of flour into a bowl and add the bicarbonate of soda, salt and mixed spice. Rub in the butter or lard, and add the sugar. Mix in the drained fruits. Make a well in the centre and put in the egg and molasses or treacle. Gradually beat the yoghurt and 150ml/5fl oz of the reserved tea into the flour to make a stiff mixture.

Put the mixture into a greased 1kg/2lbs 4oz loaf tin. Bake for 40 minutes, or until a skewer inserted in the centre comes out clean. Turn the tea bread onto a wire rack to cool.

WALNUT SODA BREAD

This is an example of how to enrich and flavour plain soda bread. Serve the loaf, either plain or buttered, with a salad or as a tasty addition to a lunch box.

MAKES ONE 500G · 1LB 2OZ LOAF

250g · 9oz wholewheat flour
½tsp bicarbonate of soda
1tsp salt
45g · 1 ½oz butter
2tbsp chopped fresh parsley
1tbsp chopped fresh thyme
45g · 1 ½oz shelled walnuts,
  finely chopped

1 medium onion, finely chopped
150ml · 5fl oz soured milk,
  cultured buttermilk, natural
  yoghurt or plain milk in
  which you have dissolved
  ½tsp cream
  of tartar

Heat the oven to 200°C/400°F/gas mark 6. Put the flour into a mixing bowl. Add the bicarbonate of soda and salt and rub in 30g/1oz butter. Add the herbs and walnuts. Soften the onion in the remaining butter in a small frying pan over a low heat, and add it to the flour mixture.

Make a well in the centre of the flour and pour in the liquid. Mix to a dough. Turn it onto a floured work surface and knead it lightly. Roll it into a round about 2.5cm/1in thick. Place the round on a floured baking sheet and score the top into eight sections.

Bake the bread for 20 minutes, or until the top is lightly browned. Lift it onto a wire rack and eat it warm or cold.

SODA BREAD

Soda bread is popular in many countries of the world, but nowhere more so than in Ireland, where both brown and white varieties fill the bakers' shops. It is easy to make and you can vary the ingredients according to availability. Soda bread is equally good with cheese and savouries as well as with sweet preserves. It is also excellent plain and buttered.

MAKES ONE 500G · 1LB 2OZ LOAF

250g · 9oz flour, either wholewheat, plain white cake flour, or a mixture – proportions according to taste
½tsp salt
½tsp bicarbonate of soda

30g · 1oz butter or lard
150ml · 5fl oz soured milk, cultured buttermilk, natural yoghurt, or plain milk in which you have dissolved ½tsp cream of tartar

Heat the oven to 200°C/400°F/gas mark 6. Put the flour into a bowl. Add the salt and bicarbonate of soda and rub in the butter or lard. Make a well in the centre and add the liquid. Mix to a dough. Turn it onto a floured board and knead it lightly. Form it into a ball and press or roll it into a round about 4cm/1 ½in thick.

Place the round on a floured baking sheet and score the top into quarters. Bake the bread for 20 minutes, or until it is just coloured and sounds hollow when tapped. Lift it onto a wire rack to cool.

Variations

Add any of the following to the flour:

1tsp dried mixed herbs or 1tbsp chopped fresh herbs.

•

½tsp caraway or cumin seeds.

•

4tbsp grated Cheddar cheese.

•

1 medium onion, chopped and softened in oil or butter.

CARROT TEA BREAD

Carrot tea bread is light and moist, with the sweetness supplied by the carrots and dried fruits as well as a small amount of sugar. Without the filling, it makes tasty lunch box fare. The addition of the filling makes it suitable for all tea-time occasions.

MAKES ONE 750G · 1 ½LB LOAF

345g · 11oz wholemeal flour
2tsp baking powder
1tsp ground cinnamon
1tsp ground nutmeg
125g · 4oz light muscovado sugar
1 large carrot, grated
60g · 2oz dried apricots, soaked, or 'no-soak' apricots

60g · 2oz sultanas
1 egg
4tbsp sunflower oil
125ml · 4fl oz carrot juice
4tbsp milk

FILLING (OPTIONAL):
60g · 2oz fromage frais
2tsp honey

Heat the oven to 180°C/350°F/gas mark 4. Put the flour into a mixing bowl. Add the baking powder, spices, sugar, carrot and dried fruits and mix together with your fingers. In a separate bowl, beat together the egg, oil, carrot juice and milk.

Make a well in the centre of the flour mixture. Pour in the liquid mixture and gradually beat it into the flour.

Spoon the mixture into a greased 1kg/2lbs 4oz loaf tin. Bake the loaf for 35 minutes, or until it is risen and golden and a skewer inserted in the centre comes out clean. Turn the tea bread onto a wire rack to cool.

To make the filling, cream the cheese in a bowl and beat in the honey. When the tea bread is cool, carefully cut the loaf crossways in two. Spread the lower half with the filling and replace the top.

Serve the loaf cut into slices.

CHAPTER FIVE

BREAD DISHES

ake a simple loaf and transform it into a complete meal. There are endless ways of using bread to create sweet or savoury dishes, or to put an interesting spin on an old and trusted favourite. You will be surprised how versatile bread is – in dishes ranging from appetisers to desserts.

BREAD DISHES

As well as forming a part of a meal – or even being a meal in itself – bread is one of the most versatile ingredients that you can find in the kitchen. With a loaf of bread, you have the basis for many sweet and savoury dishes that are easy to make and very economical.

Whether sliced, cubed or made into crumbs, bread can be used to make quick snacks, warming puddings, exciting picnics and even ice cream. For an exciting alternative to sandwiches when you go on a picnic, hollow out a loaf and fill it with a smoked mackerel terrine or a succulent mixture of tomatoes, anchovies and olive oil.

Bread can also be used for easy nursery food. Many of us may fondly remember Bread and Butter Pudding from childhood, but it can be enjoyed at any age and is well worth rediscovering. French Toast or 'eggy bread' is another childhood snack, but top it with savoury vegetables or a sweet vegetable compôte and it becomes a meal for adults, quickly prepared and inexpensive.

There are bread dishes from all over the world. In Cadiz in Spain, fresh crumbs are used to thicken Ajo, a hearty winter soup; in Italy, slices of fresh bread are brushed with olive oil or butter and baked to make crisp Crostini; and from the borders of Italy and Austria come savoury dumplings called Knödel.

A simple loaf of bread can be a passport to a wide variety of dishes.

Dos molinos, *Jacob van Ruisdael 1655*

113

AJO (GARLIC SOUP)

Ajo is a breadcrumb- and garlic-based soup that is made in the winter around Cadiz in Spain. Garlic and cayenne pepper are well known ingredients for keeping colds and flu at bay and easing their symptoms. The soup is economical and simple to make and yet very substantial. The original recipe was made only with water, but chicken stock is used here for a better flavour; if you are using a stock cube, however, choose a mild one. The soup is highly pungent and definitely for garlic lovers!

SERVES 4

100ml · 3½fl oz olive oil
5 large garlic cloves, crushed
150g · 5oz crumbs from day-old white bread
2tsp paprika
¼tsp cayenne pepper, or more if preferred

900ml · 1½pts mild chicken stock or water
2 eggs, beaten
6tbsp chopped fresh parsley

Heat the oil in a large saucepan over a low heat. Add the crushed garlic and stir for 1 minute. Add the breadcrumbs and stir continually for 10-15 minutes, or until they turn golden. Stir in the paprika and cayenne pepper. Pour in the stock or water and bring it to the boil. Cover and simmer very gently for 30 minutes, stirring occasionally.

Remove the pan from the heat and gradually beat in the eggs. Return the soup to the heat and heat gently to thicken the eggs but do not boil. Stir in the chopped parsley and serve hot.

Proverb

Stolen waters are sweet, and bread eaten in secret is pleasant.

THE BIBLE

114

KNÖDEL

Knödel come from the northern region of Alto Adige in Italy. They are light, herb-flavoured dumplings that can be served with soup or as a side dish with meat and vegetable dishes. They can be eaten plain or with melted butter and chopped sage leaves spooned over them. The original recipe contains the smoked fat called *speck*, but bacon has been substituted in the one below; it can be omitted for vegetarians or if a milder flavour is required.

Another version of *knödel*, made in the same region, is made with crumbs from a rye and buckwheat bread and the dumplings are served with *sauerkraut* (fermented cabbage) and tomato sauce.

SERVES 4

185g · 6oz breadcrumbs from day-old white bread
60g · 2oz plain white flour
4tbsp chopped parsley
1tbsp chopped marjoram
salt and freshly ground black pepper
30g · 1oz butter
1 medium onion, finely chopped

60g · 2oz fat bacon, finely chopped (optional)
100ml · 3½fl oz milk
2 eggs, beaten
1.2litres · 2pt chicken or vegetable stock

TOPPING (OPTIONAL)
45g · 1 ½oz butter
5 sage leaves, finely chopped

Combine the breadcrumbs, flour, herbs and seasoning in a large bowl. Melt the butter in a frying pan over a low heat; add the onion and bacon and cook them until the onions are soft. Stir the onion mixture into the breadcrumb mixture and mix in the milk and eggs; leave the mixture to stand and rest for 30 minutes.

Form the mixture into 8 dumplings. Pour the stock into a saucepan and bring it to the boil. Add the dumplings, cover and simmer for 20 minutes, or until they are cooked through. Lift them out with a slotted spoon onto a serving dish and keep warm.

For the topping, melt the butter in a small frying pan over a low heat. Add in the chopped sage and cook it for 30 seconds. Spoon the butter and sage over the dumplings.

BREAD SAUCE

Bread sauce is a traditional English accompaniment to roast meats and game, its mild flavour contrasting well with the richness of the meat. It developed from the medieval custom of serving sweet, breadcrumb- or almond-based puddings alongside the meat course.

SERVES 4

1 small onion
4 cloves
300ml · 10fl oz milk
½ bay leaf

60g · 2oz fresh white breadcrumbs
salt and pepper
30g · 1oz butter, cut into small pieces and softened

Peel the onion and stick the four cloves into it. Put the milk into a saucepan and bring it to the boil, but do not let it boil over. Add the onion and the bay leaf. Cover the pan, remove it from the heat and allow the milk to stand for 15 minutes to absorb the flavours.

Discard the onion. Add the breadcrumbs to the pan and season to taste. Set the pan over a low heat and bring to the boil, stirring constantly. When it begins to boil, remove the pan from the heat and discard the piece of bay leaf. Beat in the butter, one piece at a time until each piece is thoroughly incorporated. Serve hot.

Pan Bagna

Pan bagna, or *pan bagnat* as it is sometimes spelled, is the way in which 'pain baigné' (meaning 'bathed bread') is referred to in the French region of Provence. The essential ingredients are ripe tomatoes, olive oil and fresh bread; the bread is allowed to soak up the juices and become moist. Other ingredients, such as anchovies or artichoke hearts, are added according to preference. *Pan bagna* can be a meal in itself or, in smaller portions, a lunchtime snack.

SERVES 4 AS A MAIN MEAL, 6-8 AS A SNACK

1 long baguette (French loaf)	*1 mild white onion*
560g · 1lb 4 oz ripe tomatoes	*125g · 4oz tin anchovy fillets*
125ml · 4fl oz olive oil	*280g · 10oz artichoke hearts in*
1 large garlic clove, crushed	*oil*
sea salt and freshly ground	*4tbsp chopped fresh parsley*
black pepper	
125g · 4oz button mushrooms	

Slit the loaf lengthways without cutting right through. Remove all the crumb and reserve.

Scald and peel the tomatoes. Remove and reserve the seeds and juice; cut the flesh into thin strips. Place the tomato flesh in a large bowl. Add half the olive oil, all the garlic and seasonings. Crumble half the reserved crumb of the loaf and mix it into the tomato seeds and juice.

Thinly slice the mushrooms and the onion. Heat the remaining olive oil in a frying pan over a low heat. Add the onion and cook for 5 minutes, or until it is transparent. Add the mushrooms and continue cooking for a further 2 minutes, or until they are just cooked through. Remove pan from the heat and allow to cool.

Cut the anchovy fillets in half lengthways and each half into two or three pieces crossways, depending on their size. Drain and slice the artichoke hearts.

Fold the tomato-soaked bread, the mushroom mixture, the anchovies, artichoke hearts and parsley into the sliced tomato flesh.

Fill the loaf with the mixture and close. Tie the loaf in several places with string to press the sides together and wrap it in plastic film. Leave the loaf for 24 hours in a cool place so the juices soak into the crust.

Serve cut crossways into portions.

Deep-fried Bread

In all parts of the world, small pieces of raised dough are deep fried to make delectable snacks, sweet cakes or accompaniments to main meals.

In Europe and the USA, the doughnut is perhaps the best known version of deep-fried bread. The doughnuts we know today probably originated in the Scottish communities living on the borders of north-eastern USA and Canada in the middle of the nineteenth century. There, these small cakes – crisp on the outside and soft in the middle – were frequently eaten for breakfast, either plain or with maple sugar or maple syrup. Ring doughnuts were the first to become popular. The jam-filled ones were a later development and are now more frequently bought from the bakerery than made at home.

In the cities of Mexico you will find the *churria* or *churro* shop, and inside you will be able to buy freshly fried *churros* to accompany a cup of hot chocolate or the milky coffee known as *café con leche*. *Churros* are made from a type of choux pastry dough, which is piped in lengths of about 18cm/7in into lemon- flavoured hot oil and cooked until brown and crisp. To serve, they are sprinkled with aniseed-flavoured sugar.

Koeksisters are a South African speciality, which are served for dessert or as a sweet snack. Plain white flour, butter and milk are the main ingredients, together with either yeast or baking powder. The soft dough is made into thin strips which are plaited together in threes before being deep fried in hot oil. As soon as they are golden and crisp, they are lifted out of the oil and immediately plunged into an ice-cold syrup, flavoured with lemon juice and ginger. Once coated in the syrup, they are taken out and left on a wire rack to dry.

Also from South Africa are *vetkoek*, which are eaten as a snack or with meals as a substitute for bread. One version is made simply by deep frying small pieces of plain white or wholewheat bread dough until brown and crisp. Quick *vetkoek* are made by dropping spoonfuls of batter into hot oil.

If you were in Trinidad in the Caribbean and wanted to sample really local food, you would probably be directed to an establishment which sold *accra* and 'floats'. *Accra* are deep-fried fish cakes made with the local salt fish. Floats are their natural accompaniment and are made with a lard-enriched bread dough, fried in rounds which puff up in the oil.

Sugared Ring Doughnuts

Makes about 18 doughnuts

125g • 4oz sugar
15g • ½oz lard or shortening
1 egg, beaten
4 drops vanilla essence
250g • 8oz plain white flour
1tsp baking powder
¼tsp bicarbonate of soda
¼tsp salt
¼tsp ground nutmeg
180ml • 6fl oz cultured buttermilk (or milk soured with
1tsp cream of tartar)
oil for deep frying
90g • 3oz caster sugar

Put the sugar into a large mixing bowl and work in the lard or shortening. Then beat in the egg, a little at a time, and the vanilla essence. Mix the flour with the baking powder, bicarbonate of soda, salt and nutmeg. Beat it into the sugar mixture, alternately with the buttermilk, to make a very moist dough. Cover the bowl with plastic film and put it into the refrigerator for at least an hour (or overnight if the doughnuts are for breakfast) for the dough to firm. To cook, put the dough onto a floured work surface and sprinkle it with more flour. Roll it to a thickness of about 12mm/½in. Using a floured biscuit cutter, stamp the dough into 6.5cm/2½in rounds. Stamp a 12mm/½in hole in the centre of each round, again using a floured biscuit cutter, or an apple corer. Form the small circles from the middles into a ball again and roll out. Repeat until all the dough is used. Heat a pan of oil on a high heat. Sprinkle half the sugar over two pieces of kitchen paper. Put the doughnuts into the oil, about three at a time. Cook them for about 1 minute on each side, or until they are golden brown. Lift them out and place them on the kitchen paper. Sprinkle a little more sugar over the top. Eat the doughnuts warm.

Floats

Makes ten rolls

15g • ¹/₂oz fresh yeast or 2tsp dried yeast
180ml • 6fl oz warm water
250g • 8oz plain cake flour
1tsp salt
60g • 2oz lard
oil for deep frying

In a small bowl, sprinkle the yeast into half the water. Leave fresh yeast for 5 minutes and dried for 15 minutes. Put the flour into a large mixing bowl. Add the salt and rub in the lard. Make a well in the centre and pour in the yeast mixture and the remaining water. Mix to a dough. Turn the dough onto a floured work surface and knead it until it is smooth. Return it to the bowl, cover it with a clean cloth and leave it in a warm place for 45 minutes, or until it has doubled in size.
Knead the dough again and divide it into ten small balls. Place them on a floured board or baking sheet, cover them with a cloth and leave them for a further 45 minutes.
Without kneading again, roll each ball into a round 'float', about 7.5cm/3in in diameter.
Heat a pan of deep oil on a high heat. Put in the 'floats', one at a time, and cook them for about one minute on each side, until they are golden brown and puffed up.
Drain the 'floats' on kitchen paper and serve them warm, either as a snack or with a fish dish.

Quick Vetkoek

Makes about 12 small snacks

250g • 8oz strong, plain white flour
¹/₂tsp salt
1tbsp baking powder
330ml • 11fl oz milk
oil for deep frying

Put the flour into a mixing bowl and toss in the salt and baking powder. Make a well in the centre and beat in the milk to make a soft batter.
Heat the oil on a high heat. Ladle individual tablespoonfuls of the mixture into the oil and fry them for 1 minute on each side, or until they are crisp and golden. Drain the *vetkoek* on kitchen paper and eat them hot.

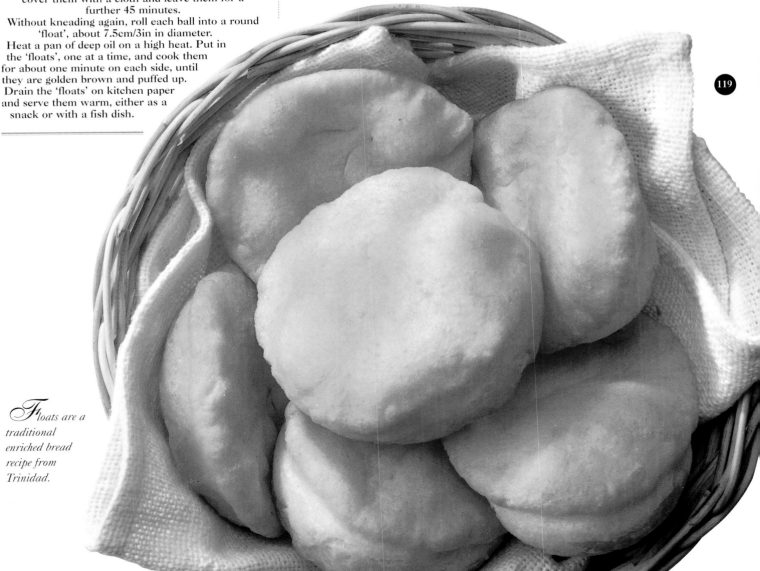

Floats are a traditional enriched bread recipe from Trinidad.

119

CROSTINI DI MARE

Crostini are pieces of bread that have been brushed with butter or oil and baked until crisp in the oven. They can be used as a base for many different kinds of food. In Italy, *Crostini di Mare*, filled with seafood, are a popular snack. As a main meal, serve them with green vegetables or a salad.

SERVES 4

*4 slices bread cut from a
    bloomer-type loaf,
    5cm · 2in thick*
90g · 3oz butter
375g · 13oz firm white fish

*125g · 4oz fresh, uncooked
    shelled prawns*
juice ½ lemon
4tbsp chopped fresh parsley

Heat the oven to 200°C/400°F/gas mark 6. Using a small sharp knife, cut round about 12mm/½in in from the crust of each slice of bread, taking the cut to within 12mm/½in of the base. Carefully remove the centre crumb, making a bread cup about 12mm/½in thick. Reserve 30g/1oz of the scooped out centres and make it into fine crumbs. Melt 60g/2oz of the butter and use it to brush the cups inside and out. Lay them on a baking sheet and place them in the oven for about 7 minutes, or until they are crisp and golden. Keep them warm.

Cut the fish into 12mm/½in cubes. Melt the remaining butter in a large frying pan over a high heat. Add the fish and prawns and stir them for about 2 minutes, or until they are cooked through. Remove them and keep them warm. Add the reserved crumbs to the pan and stir them until they turn golden. Return the fish and prawns to the pan. Stir in the lemon juice and bring to a simmer; stir in the parsley. Remove the pan from the heat and spoon the mixture into the prepared *crostini*. Serve warm.

FRENCH TOAST

French toast is also called by the fond nursery name of 'eggy bread'. In times of food shortages, it was a way of making one egg spread a long way. It is also an economical way of producing a rich base for both sweet and savoury snacks. French toast should be golden and crisp on the outside and light and airy in the middle.

BASIC RECIPE SERVES 4

4 slices medium-cut white bread
2 eggs
salt and pepper (for savoury
    meals only)

pinch of spice (optional); use
    different spices for sweet or
    savoury serving
up to 60g · 2oz butter

Cut the crusts from the bread and cut each slice in half. Beat the eggs in a shallow dish. Add the seasonings, if using. Dip the slices of bread in the beaten egg.

Melt half the butter in a frying pan over a medium heat. Put in as many slices of bread as the pan will take and fry them for about 2 minutes on each side, or until they are golden brown and crisp. Cook the remaining pieces of bread in the same way, adding more butter as you need it. Serve each slice hot.

Savoury Toppings

Try serving savoury french toast with baked beans, grated cheese, grilled tomato slices, grilled mushrooms, crispy bacon, sausages, cold meats, vegetable casseroles, mixtures of grilled or roasted vegetables, or salads.

Sweet Toppings

Delicious alternatives include jam or preserves, honey, cinnamon sugar (made by keeping a cinnamon stick in a jar of caster sugar), vanilla sugar (made by keeping a vanilla pod in a jar of caster sugar), maple syrup, stewed fruit and tinned or bottled fruit.

LAYERED SMOKED MACKEREL LOAF

Hollowed-out loaves make ideal containers for other food and are perfect for outdoor eating. This one is filled with a simply made terrine of smoked mackerel. The ideal loaf for this recipe is one that you have made yourself from the basic bread recipe (page 30) and baked in a 1kg/2lbs 4oz bread tin. A lot of crumbs result from this filled loaf, which you can use for many of the other recipes in this section. Serve the loaf for a lunch or for a special picnic.

SERVES 6

1 white or wholewheat loaf
    baked in a 1kg · 2lbs 4oz
    bread tin
30g · 1oz butter
750g · 1 ½lb smoked mackerel
    fillets
350g · 12oz curd cheese or
    fromage frais

grated rind and juice 1 lemon
2tbsp preserved grated
    horseradish
2tbsp tomato purée
1tsp Tabasco sauce
60g · 2oz parsley, finely
    chopped

Slice the rounded top off the loaf. Remove all the inside of the loaf, leaving a shell about 1cm/½in thick. Butter the inside. Hollow out the top and butter the lower side.

Skin and bone the smoked mackerel fillets. Reserve 185g/6oz. Flake the remainder and put them into a bowl; pound them with a heavy wooden spoon to break them up even further. Gradually beat in the cheese and then the lemon rind and juice, horseradish, tomato purée and Tabasco sauce. Cut the reserved pieces of mackerel into thin strips.

Put one quarter of the pâté mixture into the bottom of the hollowed loaf. Scatter half the parsley on top in an even layer. Add a further quarter of the mixture. Lay all the strips of mackerel on top, running lengthways along the loaf. Add another quarter of the mixture and top with the remaining parsley. Add the remaining mixture. It should come just above the sides of the loaf. Put on the top and wrap the loaf in polythene film.

Refrigerate the loaf for 1 hour. Serve it cut into slices about 2.5cm/1in thick.

BREADCRUMB STUFFING

Different types of breadcrumb stuffing are used in all areas of the world for meats, poultry and vegetables such as marrow or sweet peppers. The basic recipe is always the same; it is the additions, such as herbs or perhaps small amounts of vegetables, that vary the flavours considerably. Stuffings can be made from white, wholewheat or mixed grain breads, depending on availability and your own personal preferences.

BASIC RECIPE SERVES 4-6

*30g · 1oz butter or 4tbsp
    vegetable oil
1 medium onion, finely chopped
    or thinly sliced as preferred
125g · 4oz fresh breadcrumbs*

*4tbsp liquid (stock, dry red or
    white wine or cider)
1tsp dried or 2tbsp chopped
    fresh herbs
seasoning*

Melt the butter or heat the oil in a frying pan over a low heat. Put in the onion and soften it. With the pan still over the heat, add the breadcrumbs, the liquid and the herbs, and mix together and season.

If the stuffing is for meat of any kind, cool it completely before using.

Variations

Herbs

Suggested herb accompaniments include:

With goose and lamb, try 4 chopped sage leaves.

•

With chicken, game, lamb and turkey, add 1tbsp each of chopped thyme and marjoram.

•

Lamb is delicious with 1tbsp chopped thyme and 1tsp chopped rosemary.

•

Pork works well with 2 chopped sage leaves and 1tsp chopped rosemary.

•

Try 2tbsp chopped chervil with chicken.

•

With chicken, lamb and turkey, try 1tbsp chopped tarragon.

Vegetables

The following vegetable suggestions should be cooked with the onion in the frying pan for the best result:

When cooking lamb, try adding 1 chopped garlic clove.

•

With game or poultry, add 60g/2oz chopped or sliced mushrooms for a tasty option.

•

For an unusual variation, try ¼ chopped fennel bulb with game, lamb, pork and poultry.

•

Adding 1 sweet red or green pepper, seeded and chopped, makes a tasty addition to chicken and lamb.

Spices

Add small amounts of the following spices to give a special flavour to the stuffing:

Ground or crushed allspice with chicken, duck, goose, lamb and pork.

•

Try ground cloves with duck, goose and lamb.

•

With duck, game, goose and pork, try crushed juniper berries.

•

Try ground mace to accompany chicken, game, lamb and turkey.

Nuts

Add small amounts of the following nuts for texture and taste, but beware of any nut allergies:

Try 60g/2oz chopped walnuts or 60g/2oz cooked and sliced chestnuts with meat and vegetarian dishes.

•

Also delicious is 60g/2oz chopped brazil nuts with vegetarian dishes.

Fruits

These fruits make a fresh and interesting change. They should be cooked with the onion in the frying pan:

With lamb and pork, try 3 plums, stoned and chopped.

•

Chicken and duck are complemented by adding 60g/2oz whole redcurrants.

•

A traditional alternative is to add 1 small cooking apple, peeled, cored and chopped, with goose and pork.

CHEESE *and* BACON CAKE

This Spanish bread pudding is savoury. It originated in La Mancha, a barren plateau in central Spain, and the cheese used locally is made from the milk of the hardy Manchego breed of sheep. The cheese, called *manchego*, is a pressed, uncooked, curd cheese with a slightly salty flavour. Where this is unobtainable, feta cheese makes a good substitute. White, thick-sliced bread works best in this recipe. Cheese and bacon Cake is very rich and, accompanied by a salad, makes an excellent lunch or supper dish.

Heat the oven to 180°C/350°F/gas mark 4. Cut the bread into small cubes and put them into the bottom of a 1.2litre/2pt pie dish. Beat the eggs in a bowl. Beat in the *manchego* or feta cheese and the milk; season to taste. Pour the mixture over the bread.

Stand the pie dish in a baking tray half filled with water. Bake the cake for 15 minutes. Then place the bacon slices over the top of the cake and continue cooking for a further 20 minutes, or until the pudding is risen and set. Serve sliced either hot or warm.

SERVES 4

4 slices thick-cut white bread
3 eggs
155g • 5oz manchego or feta cheese, crumbled

560ml • 18fl oz milk
salt and freshly ground black pepper
4 slices streaky bacon

CHRISTMAS PUDDING

Christmas Pudding is another medieval dish. Like bread sauce, it originates from a breadcrumb-based pudding containing dried fruits and spices that was served alongside roast meats. The original pudding had a texture resembling bread sauce, rather than the denser, heavier 'cake' of today. The pudding below is made from wholewheat breadcrumbs, flour and dark sugar and is packed with dried fruits. The list of ingredients may look daunting, but the recipe is incredibly easy to make.

SERVES 8

60g · 2oz whole dried apricots
60g · 2oz stoned dates
60g · 2oz currants
90g · 3oz raisins
90g · 3oz sultanas
60g · 2oz candied peel (in the piece and chopped)
85ml · 2 ½fl oz dark stout or porter
85ml · 2 ½fl oz brandy
30g · 1oz flaked almonds
1 small cooking apple

60g · 2oz dark muscovado sugar
60g · 2oz fresh wholewheat breadcrumbs
60g · 2oz wholewheat flour
60g · 2oz vegetable suet
½tsp baking powder
pinch salt
¼ nutmeg, grated
½tsp ground cinnamon
1 egg, beaten
butter for greasing

Finely chop the apricots and dates. Put them into a bowl and mix in the currants, raisins, sultanas and candied peel. Pour in the stout or porter and the brandy. Cover with a clean cloth and leave the fruits to soak for 24 hours.

The next day, crush the almond flakes slightly and add to the fruits. Peel and core the apple and grate it into the bowl. Mix in the sugar, breadcrumbs, flour, vegetable suet, baking powder and salt. Add the spices and beaten egg. Stir everything together and make a wish!

Spoon the mixture into a buttered, 900ml/1½pt pudding basin. Cover the top with a circle of buttered greaseproof paper and then a circle of foil, both about 5cm/2in larger than the top of the basin. Tie them down with string and make a handle with a couple of loops for easy lifting.

Place a trivet in the bottom of a large saucepan. Pour in enough water to come about three quarters up the sides of the bowl when it is standing on the trivet. Bring the water to the boil and lower in the pudding. Cover the pan tightly and steam the pudding for 4 hours, topping up the water with boiling water from the kettle when necessary. Do not allow the saucepan to boil dry.

When ready, lift out the pudding. Remove the greaseproof and foil covering to allow it to cool completely. When cold, replace the two coverings and tie on tightly.

On Christmas morning, steam the pudding in the same way for a further 2 hours, or, alternatively, you can microwave it for 4 minutes but remember to remove the foil covering first.

Note: To flame a Christmas pudding. Just before serving, turn it onto a warmed serving dish. Pour about 3tbsp brandy into a ladle and hold the ladle over a candle flame for about 1 minute for the brandy to warm. Light the brandy while it is still in the ladle and immediately pour it over the pudding where it will burn with a pretty blue flame.

Brown Bread *and* Honey
Ice Cream

Brown bread ice cream makes a delicious dessert in either summer or winter. It is based on a simple vanilla ice cream recipe and contains crunchy breadcrumbs which have been caramelised with sugar. The trick in making it is to add the breadcrumbs at the last minute and only when the ice cream is almost frozen so that they do not soak up too much liquid, and so retain their crunch.

MAKES APPROXIMATELY 1 LITRE · 1 ¾ PINTS

125g · 4oz fresh wholewheat breadcrumbs
3tbsp golden granulated sugar
2 eggs
2 egg yolks
90g · 3oz honey

500ml · 18fl oz full cream milk
250ml · 9fl oz double cream
1 vanilla pod, or 3 drops vanilla essence

Heat the oven to 180°C/350°F/gas mark 4. Place the breadcrumbs in a shallow baking tin and scatter the sugar over them. Bake the breadcrumbs in the oven for 5 minutes. Remove the tin, and break up and stir the breadcrumb mixture. Return the tin to the oven for a further 5 minutes until the breadcrumbs are golden brown and crisp. Break the mixture up again and tip it immediately onto a cool, heatproof plate.

Beat the eggs and egg yolks with the honey, either by hand or with an electric whisk, until the mixture is pale and frothy. Pour the milk and cream into a saucepan with the vanilla pod or vanilla essence and bring to just below boiling point. Remove the pan from the heat and discard the vanilla pod, if using. Whip the milk mixture into the egg yolks and honey in a thin, steady stream. Allow the mixture to cool.

Spoon the mixture into a freezing tray and place it in the coldest part of the freezer for 3 hours, taking it out every 30 minutes to stir it so that it freezes evenly. The last time you do this, mix in the breadcrumbs.

If you are using an ice cream-maker, follow the manufacturer's instructions for vanilla ice cream and add the breadcrumbs when the mixture is almost frozen. Allow the ice cream to freeze completely. It can be served immediately or can be packed into a container, covered and placed in the freezer for storage.

Bread *and* Butter Pudding

Bread and butter pudding is a traditional English dessert that originally was baked for a long time in the slow oven of the kitchen range. It should be light and fluffy in texture and crisp and brown on top. Wholemeal bread is used in the recipe below but you can also use white bread for a lighter result. An ordinary medium-cut sliced loaf works best.

SERVES 6

45g · 1 ½oz butter, softened
4 slices medium-cut wholewheat bread
60g · 2oz raisins
60g · 2oz sultanas
grated rind ½ lemon

3tbsp golden granulated sugar
freshly grated nutmeg, about ⅛ of a nut
2 eggs
1 egg yolk
600ml · 1pt full cream milk

Heat the oven to 180°C/350°F/gas mark 4. Butter the bread slices generously and cut them into triangular quarters. In a bowl, mix together the raisins, sultanas and lemon rind.

Arrange one-third of the bread slices in the bottom of a 900ml/1½pt pie dish. Scatter them with half the dried fruit mixture and 1tbsp of the sugar. Grate over a little nutmeg. Repeat the layers. Top with the remaining bread slices, the remaining sugar and remaining grated nutmeg. Beat together the eggs, egg yolk and milk. Pour the egg mixture over the contents of the pie dish.

Stand the pie dish in a baking tray half-filled with water. Bake the pudding for 30 minutes, or until it is light and risen and the top is golden brown. It is delicious served both warm with custard or cream, and cold and sliced.

INDEX *of* RECIPES

127

CREDITS

Quarto would like to thank the following for providing photographs and
for permission to reproduce copyright material. While every effort has
been made to trace and acknowledge all copyright holders, we would like
to apologise should any omissions have been made.

Key: *t* top, *c* centre, *b* below, *r* right, *l* left

ACE Photo Agency 11 *bl* (Keith Eager), 14 *bl* (Paul Thompson); AKG
London 39; Axiom 20 *bl*; e.t.archive 13 *br*; Image Bank 18 *bl*; Image
Select 9 *br*; 21 *br* (Ann Ronan), 57, 17 *tr* (C.F.C.L.), 17; Impact 14 *tr*
(Caroline Penn), 15 *tr* Marcus Pietrek; Life File 7 *tr* (Mike Maidment), 13
tl (Sergei Verein), 87 (Andrew Ward); North Wind Picture Archive 7 *br*, 8
bl, 10 *tl*, 10 *bl*, 11 *tr*, 16 *bl*, 17 *br*, 41, 103; Pictor 16 *tl*; Tony Stone 6, 15 *b*,
66 *b*, 69; Travel Ink 19 (Steve Hines); Visual Arts Library 8 *tl* (Artophot),
18 *tr*, 97, 113 (National Gallery, London. Photo Joseph Martin/VAL).

All other photographs are the copyright of Quarto Publishing plc.

Index by Susan M. Cawthorne